SEA, ICE
and
ROCK

SEA, ICE
and
ROCK

Sailing and Climbing
Above the Arctic Circle

CHRIS BONINGTON AND ROBIN KNOX-JOHNSTON

Vertebrate Publishing, Sheffield
www.v-publishing.co.uk

Sea, Ice and Rock

Chris Bonington and Robin Knox-Johnston

 Vertebrate Publishing
Omega Court, 352 Cemetery Road, Sheffield S11 8FT, United Kingdom.
www.v-publishing.co.uk

First published in Great Britain and the United States in 1993 by Hodder
and Stoughton (Kent) and Sheridan House Inc. (New York). This edition first
published in 2020 by Vertebrate Publishing.

Vertebrate Publishing
Omega Court, 352 Cemetery Road, Sheffield S11 8FT

Cover image: *Suhaili*. Photo: Chris Bonington.
Photography by the authors unless otherwise accredited.

Maps drawn by Linda Blakemore.

This book is a work of non-fiction based on the life, experiences and
recollections of Chris Bonington and Robin Knox-Johnston. In some limited
cases the names of people, places, dates and sequences or the detail of events
have been changed solely to protect the privacy of others. The authors have
stated to the publishers that, except in such minor respects not affecting the
substantial accuracy of the work, the contents of the book are true.

A CIP catalogue record for this book is available from the British Library.

978-1-912560-53-0 (Ebook)
978-1-912560-52-3 (Paperback)

Produced by Vertebrate Publishing.

Also by Chris Bonington

I Chose to Climb
Annapurna South Face
The Next Horizon
Everest South West Face
Everest the Hard Way
Quest for Adventure
Kongur China's Elusive Summit
Everest the Unclimbed Ridge
(with Charles Clarke)
The Everest Years
Mountaineer
The Climbers

Also by Robin Knox-Johnston

A World of My Own
Sailing
Last But Not Least
The Twilight of Sail
Seamanship
The Boc Challenge 1986-87
(with Barry Pickthall)
The Cape of Good Hope
The History of Yachting
The Columbus Venture

Contents

1 A Greenland Invitation

It started, as most expeditions do, with a phone call. I was in New Zealand and, when I rang home one day, my wife Wendy told me that Robin Knox-Johnston had just called to ask whether I was interested in sailing to Greenland with him and then taking him up a climb. At that stage I was thinking of going climbing in the Tien Shan, in what was then the Soviet Union, but there was something so refreshingly different about this proposal, that I asked Wendy to accept the invitation on my behalf.

I had first met Robin in the autumn of 1978 on a charity edition of the television show *The Krypton Factor*. This consisted of a series of challenges that were designed to test physical stamina, practical and mental ingenuity and general knowledge. There were four competitors, Ranulph Fiennes, the polar adventurer, Robin Knox-Johnston, first man to sail around the world non-stop single-handed, Don Cameron, the balloonist, and me. We first met on a bleak army assault course on the Lancashire moors. I thought I had it weighed up. Fiennes, tall, lean, and ex-SAS, was almost certain to beat me, but I should come an easy second. Neither a sailor nor a balloonist should be able to keep up with a mountaineer. It was a straight race, with the four of us starting together. Fiennes pulled away easily but Robin was on his tail. I thought I'd catch up with my mountaineer's stamina telling in the end, but the gap widened and I came in a poor third, my ego severely dented. I consoled myself with the fact that I was still in poor shape following a fall on the Ogre in the Karakoram the previous year. My confidence was restored in the cerebral part of the test when I managed to redeem myself, becoming the overall winner.

I met Robin again a year later when I was researching a book which I called *Quest for Adventure*. It was a study of post-war adventure in all its aspects. I rang to ask for an interview and he told me he was about to go cruising round the Western Isles with his family on his yacht, *Suhaili*. He suggested instead of just interviewing him we might exchange skills. He'd teach me something about sailing and I could take him climbing. We arranged to meet at Oban and I drove up in July 1979.

It didn't start too well. I went to the wrong part of the harbour, and was late anyway, having combed the Oban shops for a map of the Cuillin Ridge in Skye which was to be our land objective. I had forgotten to bring my own. Eventually I located a half-inch to the mile map, which would hardly be adequate for the intricate navigation required on the Cuillin, and then found *Suhaili* at the far end of the harbour. Robin and Sue, with their daughter Sara, were pleasantly relaxed about my late arrival and we set sail, or rather began motoring, as soon as I had brought my gear aboard. It was difficult to believe that Robin had sailed this small, 32-foot ketch round the world single-handed, through the Roaring Forties, and that on one occasion, when a huge rogue wave had swept it while he was working up forward, his only means of saving himself had been to climb the shrouds and cling to the main mast as the boat disappeared in roaring waters and foam. Chugging up the Sound of Mull, sipping a gin and tonic, was a far cry from that.

We anchored for the night in a small bay and the next day reached Loch Scavaig on Skye. I was already captivated by this style of sailing as I was seeing the hills of the Highlands from a different perspective and the very slowness of our progress was a bonus. It gave time to savour their changing aspect as we crept round Muck and Eigg, passed Rhum on the port side, and saw the jagged ramparts of the Cuillin loom ever higher.

The anchorage was a small bay, barely protected by a rocky peninsula. That evening, while Sue cooked supper, Robin rowed me ashore and I gave him his first taste of rock climbing on a little crag just above the bay. It was probably a new route, taking a diagonal line up steep rough gabbro. When he came to follow me, I could see he wasn't a natural climber. His movement was slow and awkward, yet quietly determined. Even though the rope was at an angle and the climb on the hard side for a total beginner, he coped with it in a calm methodical way and was obviously enjoying it.

The next morning we set out for our expedition on to the main ridge, walking up the side of Loch Coruisk and then up the ridge of the Dubhs, padding over the smooth black gabbro boiler plates, which swept up into a low cloud base. I had forgotten the Dubh Gap, a vertical step on the ridge, down which you need to abseil. I did at least have a rope, produced it from my rucksack, dropped the doubled ends down and started to explain to Robin the technique of abseiling.

'You know, Chris, I think it would be much better if I did this the way I'm used to. This is how I go up and down the mast.'

He rigged the ropes as a pulley round the karabiner and prepared to set off. I didn't like the idea at all.

'Look, I'm responsible if anything goes wrong. I think you should do it as a proper abseil.'

But Robin was adamant, and lowered himself down as if he was in a bosun's chair. I was immensely relieved when he reached the bottom and I was able to follow him down.

We were now in thick cloud approaching the crest of the ridge. The map I had bought in Oban was useless and I was uncomfortably aware of how easy it was to take the wrong turning. As we stumbled on I was getting more and more worried but determined not to let Robin know of my doubts. We met up with two other climbers, the first we had seen that day, and I tried in the course of our conversation to find out exactly where we were without letting on that I was totally lost. Luckily, I discovered we were still on the main ridge and going in the right direction.

After a short scramble we reached the Thearlaich Dubh Gap, a gash out of the ridge which once again called for an abseil. Robin did it his way. On the other side of the gap is *King's Chimney*, a short climb with water dripping down it, making the rock slippery. Robin had a struggle but arrived at the top grinning, muttering that climbing the mast of *Suhaili* was more his style. I was enjoying myself on this wild mountain day in the swirling clouds with glimpses of dark craggy rock below and around us, and my pleasure was enhanced by introducing and sharing a skill and experience that meant so much to me. The wind was getting stronger, gusting round the pinnacles of the ridge crest and I could see that Robin was worried. *Suhaili's* anchorage was open to the south and he was afraid the anchor might drag. We dropped down a side gully to reach the valley and returned by the shore of Loch Coruisk to the boat.

The following morning, sailing past the Isle of Rhum, we came across the Royal Yacht. Robin hurriedly hoisted an ensign so that we could dip it and radioed loyal greetings. Then he dropped me off at Tobermory and continued his holiday, while I went home to continue writing my book. I was so taken with offshore sailing that I started talking of buying a boat. But Wendy was more realistic, asking me how I would cope with all the maintenance and everything. So sailing remained a delightful one-off experience and, though we didn't meet up again, Robin and I had built the foundation of a very real friendship. His proposal that we should sail to Greenland was an extension, on a rather grand scale, of our voyage to Skye.

As soon as I got home from New Zealand I started researching a suitable climbing objective and quickly discovered that the most interesting and dramatic unclimbed mountains were on Greenland's forbidding east coast, but that this was also the most difficult to reach by boat. I was told we would be mad to try to take *Suhaili* into its ice-locked fjords. While Robin read the *Admiralty Pilot* and thought positively around its blunt warnings in order to select us a possible anchorage, I combed expedition reports and made phone calls and found everyone kept referring me to a young climber called Jim Lowther who, I discovered, lived on my own doorstep. He came over from Penrith to see me, carrying a case full of maps, photographs and reports. Although only twenty-five years old, he had been to Greenland on ten different occasions, starting with school expeditions and going on to organise his own. A few days later he called to let me know he had the ideal objective, a peak he had seen from a distance the previous summer on an expedition to explore and climb in the Watkins Range. The mountain, named the Cathedral, was situated in the Lemon Mountains, a range visited by Lawrence Wager in 1936. Stan Woolley, another inveterate Greenland hand, went there in 1972, but no one had been there since and it remained unclimbed.

Jim came over the following night and showed me some pictures of the Cathedral. It looked superb, a wedge-like pyramid of snow and rock, that reminded me a little of the Aiguille Verte in the Mont Blanc massif. Jim assured me that the rock was granite and that Stan Woolley had described the Cathedral as 'the most attractive and challenging unclimbed peak in Greenland'.

It sounded great, but could we get there? The peak was near the head of a fjord called Kangerdlugssuaq, about halfway between Angmagssalik and Scoresby Sound, tucked into a gigantic open corner that apparently tended to hold the floe ice, so that in some years it was impossible, or at least very difficult, to get in to the coast. But my imagination was caught and I recommended to Robin that this should be our objective.

By this time I was getting to know Jim Lowther better. We had been ice climbing on Helvellyn and I was impressed by his competence and modesty. I had decided I needed another experienced climber in the team, since Robin was a novice, and Jim seemed an ideal choice. Although he was only a little older than my own elder son, I never felt the difference in age. He has a very mature approach to life and yet a real sense of fun and adventure. He certainly has his share of responsibility. Third son of the Earl of Lonsdale, one of the biggest landowners in the Lake District, he was helping to manage the complex and multi-faceted businesses of the Lowther Estate. In the following months I came to appreciate his reliability. If I asked him to do anything, he got on with the job quickly and efficiently, assembling the pulks (or sledges) that we planned to manhaul to the foot of the mountain, sorting out our rations and gleaning as much information as possible about the area.

Robin, meanwhile, was busy preparing *Suhaili* and planning the voyage. He takes up the story.

Once I received the news that Chris was available for the expedition, there were two urgent matters which required attention. Firstly, so Chris could choose a suitable objective, it was necessary to study Greenland's coast in detail to select potential landing places. Secondly *Suhaili,* my twenty-eight-year-old, 32-foot Bermudan ketch, had to be made ready and a crew selected.

Chris and I agreed our objective should be on or near the largely inaccessible east coast. This inaccessibility is due to the pack ice which makes navigation complex and dangerous. However, as this is why there are many unclimbed mountains close to the shore, we could hardly complain.

The *Admiralty Pilot* describes the coast as follows:

'The east coast of Greenland extends from Kap Farvel (59° 46' N 43° 55' W) in the south to Kap Morris Jesup in the north, less than 400 miles from the North Pole. The principal settlements on the coast of Greenland are at Angmagssalik and Scoresby Sund.

The whole of this immense length of coastline is fronted by a huge belt of ice of varying width, and it must be remembered that the fjords, bays and channels are in most cases completely frozen over from shore to shore during some part of the year. There are still great stretches of coast which have never yet been approached in a surface vessel, and our knowledge of them has been obtained either by voyages in boats or native craft along the partly ice-free zone between the land and sea ice, by aircraft reconnaissance, or by means of sledging journeys over the ice fringing the land.'

It was reasonable therefore to suppose that in some areas the pack ice does disperse briefly, but even the major settlement at Scoresby Sound, where there are tidal flows to aid the clearance of ice from the entrance, is not open every year. Further north, where the land is largely unmapped, the ice was almost certain to be impenetrable. To the south of Scoresby there were really only two fjords which might afford shelter for the boat, Kangerdlugssuaq and Angmagssalik. The latter was reachable, but this meant some of its mountains had already been climbed. The former was attractive, especially as it is seldom visited and there are no detailed charts. The disadvantage was that the ice does not always break up sufficiently to allow entry, but on average there was a good chance of a passage through in August. So I proposed Kangerdlugssuaq to Chris as the prime possibility, followed by Scoresby and then Angmagssalik in case Kangerdlugssuaq was not feasible. Very soon afterwards he and Jim Lowther found the Cathedral, and our destination was finalised.

Kangerdlugssuaq is the second largest fjord on the south-eastern coast of Greenland and the entrance lies at 68° 08' N, just inside the Arctic Circle. It extends forty miles north-north-west into the interior with two branch fjords, Amdrup and Watkins, leading off to the west-north-west and east respectively, quite near to the entrance. The *Pilot* refers to an anchorage near the entrance at Uttental Sound, but there also appeared to be a good spot for a small boat just at the southern end of Kraemer Island. The most recent navigation report is dated 1941 and states that both branch fjords are congested with ice and very large icebergs almost block the approaches. We could bypass the icebergs, but tightly packed ice would pose an insoluble problem. Overall the information in the *Pilot* was general and limited, and the Danish Navy charts of Kangerdlugssuaq showed only white for the upper reaches, indicating there was no data for this area.

The weather conditions in the Denmark Strait between Iceland and Greenland are often stormy, although the percentage of gales for July is only ten. Fog would be more of a worry, and as *Suhaili* is not fitted with radar, this could be particularly serious in conjunction with sea ice or icebergs. The winds in the fjords can be ferocious, caused by cold air funnelling down from the vast Greenland Icecap, and may reach hurricane strength. The effect is local, only a few miles away it can be calm, but I noted their frequency increased rapidly from September onwards, along with depressions over Iceland, so it seemed prudent to plan to be well south by the end of August at the latest.

Chris acquired a map compiled from an aerial survey which was on a larger scale than the chart and included both Kangerdlugssuaq Fjord and the Cathedral. It showed our direct route to be via the Courtauld Glacier, but as this is some way up the main fjord, it would probably be inaccessible by boat. So we also considered the Sidegletscher, off Watkins Fjord, which was more likely to be navigable, but would entail a rather longer land journey of about forty miles to our mountain. If Watkins Fjord was not viable, there was one final alternative, the neighbouring Mikis Fjord, but this would add a further three days to the trek.

Apart from dodging icebergs in the Southern Ocean while competing in a Whitbread Round the World Race, I had never sailed through ice. I needed information about its approximate location, thickness and movement. However, the moment I made enquiries, I learned how jealously guarded are Greenland's secrets. Happily, this seemed to apply more to landsmen than sea-men, and one or two friends who had sailed north of the Arctic Circle sent their reports which were very valuable. Unfortunately, none had stayed in the fjords for longer than a few days and none had visited the Kangerdlugssuaq region. Bill Tilman's books were a useful overall guide but, in his five voyages to the area, he lost one boat off Jan Mayen Island, his crew refused to proceed far beyond Iceland on another, and he lost a second boat near Angmagssalik during a subsequent trip. Ice was not a significant factor in these incidents but, if nothing else, they told me why he landed in trouble. If he had carried reliable engines and more experienced crew, many of his difficulties could have been averted. Tilman's experience also warned us that the pack ice could block the entrance to Angmagssalik right into August, although an offshore wind would often create leads through which we might penetrate. The best authority on sailing in Arctic waters was still William Scoresby in his account of whaling in the 1820s. Clear and lucid, it graphically recounted how wooden whalers manoeuvred in the pack ice, used it for shelter in storms and how on occasions they were forced to move swiftly to avoid being crushed. This gave food for thought, because if a 400-ton whaler could be damaged by the ice, it was certainly essential for a ten-ton yacht to be particularly vigilant.

Of the less helpful people, those lacking sea-going knowledge were firmly of the view that I should not embark on this venture unless accompanied by a Greenland expert. One person even suggested that I had no right to risk a boat as historic as *Suhaili* on anything so foolhardy. But I am of the view that a boat is all the better for being used and she is properly maintained if she is frequently at sea. Jim Lowther wanted me to take his Greenland hunting friend to see us through the ice, but while I welcomed the idea of having such an interesting person on board, I was adamant about not allowing him charge of my boat. In the event he refused to go in before 8th August and I believed it would be an error to wait this late, especially as Chris reckoned we needed at least two weeks ashore, and I wished to be on the way home before the end of the month, when the ferocious winds set in. On balance, I decided to ignore much of the gratuitous advice. As an island race we like to regard ourselves as a nation of seamen, but in reality there are very few professionals left, and a vast misunderstanding of the work and knowledge required to become one. A friend once said a Master's Certificate may not be an academic qualification, but it needs a minimum of seven and a half years' sea time and the equivalent study for a Master's degree.

One organisation could not be disregarded however, and this was the Danish Polar Institute. Greenland was originally a colony of Denmark and is now an integral part of Denmark with its own parliament which legislates on its internal affairs, while the Danish government is responsible for its defence and foreign policy. The Danish Polar Institute handles all applications by expeditions to climb, explore or carry out scientific work in Greenland. Since they accept the responsibility of rescuing anyone who gets into trouble, they not only insist that all expeditions are covered by a generous rescue insurance, they also vet the plans of would-be expeditioners and turn down any they feel are unjustifiably risky. Chris applied for permission for our expedition to sail to Greenland waters, and after a long delay they replied that *Suhaili* was unsuitable and therefore refused their consent. I knew that the authorities could not prevent my sailing north if I wished, many others had done so, though they might be able to bar us from landing and going inland. But they made a tactical mistake by specifying that *Suhaili* was unsuitable, since she is proven to be one of the toughest little yachts afloat. I telephoned Robin Duchesne, the Secretary General of the Royal Yachting Association. He kindly contacted his opposite number in Denmark who then explained matters to the Polar Institute and permission was granted. By now I was becoming thoroughly disillusioned with all so-called Greenland experts and bureaucracy, and concluded the best solution was to sail and deal with any problems as they arose.

For *Suhaili's* crew I needed two hands sufficiently responsible to have charge of a watch at sea and my most treasured possession for a fortnight when I was off climbing. They also had to be congenial. Congeniality may be defined in a number of ways, but for crew I mean competent, hard-working, willing, plus a good sense of humour. There is nothing worse than confining several people in a small boat who do not get on, and good humour overcomes most situations. It is difficult to find people who can take two months' holiday and have free weekends beforehand to assist with preparations. Luckily one of my regular coasting crew, Perry Crickmere, who like me served in the Merchant Navy, was so keen on the project that he persuaded his employers, a firm of London insurance brokers, to allow him the necessary leave. Short and solid at thirty-one years old, Perry has a drooping moustache and rolls his own cigarettes. I was delighted by his enthusiasm, particularly as, apart from his skill at cigarette-rolling, he is very able and practical. The other place proved harder to fill, but a paragraph in the Royal Cruising Club's newsletter, inserted by James Burdett stating he wanted a passage north between the middle of July and early September, caught my eye. The dates seemed suspiciously convenient, but they were genuine as they coincided with his vacation from law school. I liked James immediately, he has a dry sense of humour and is so laid back he is almost horizontal, but he fulfilled all my requirements, and at twenty-three was the baby of the crew. As matters turned out, I had made excellent choices.

Suhaili was completely refitted after her pasting in the Atlantic in 1989; new masts and rigging and a smart paint job. My only concern was for the eighteen-year-old engine. I was well accustomed to its foibles and could usually get it running, but sometimes this was a lengthy process, and judging from Tilman's accounts, time could be critical. Matters came to a head when, in February 1991, it began spewing out vast quantities of white smoke during the annual St Katharine's Frostbite Race. This was diagnosed as a split cylinder-head gasket, but in reality was a cracked cylinder liner. Putting a new liner into an old engine seemed rather like new wine in old skins, and in any case I had by now lost confidence in it. I contacted Perkins in Peterborough and they examined the installation. After a second visit they announced that one of the new Prima range engines was ready, but I would have to install it. Wisely, they also suggested that I attend a maintenance course before the engine was delivered.

As I had removed the engine on three previous occasions, the absence of a crane was not a problem. Perry, James and I rigged sheerlegs and lifted it out through the main hatch. The new engine, although developing eighteen extra horsepower, was conveniently slightly smaller and so went in quite easily. As a part of Perkins' service they checked the propeller size and advised we fit a new three-bladed model instead of the two-bladed one which had been with the boat since she was built. The overall results were spectacular and led to us having sufficient power to punch through a head sea in a force 6, whereas previously this was almost unachievable in force 4. Unfortunately, this all took weeks, and preparation time was further reduced when I became Managing Director of St Katharine's Haven next door to the Tower of London at the beginning of May. Chris and I had planned to have a week skiing and climbing, but this never happened. The best I managed was to spend an evening with the Royal Marine Reserves in Bermondsey where Corporal Dave Hill coached me in the basics of abseiling and jumaring.

In April we dried out along the bank of the Thames, did some caulking and gave *Suhaili* a good coat of anti-fouling. We were still debating how to protect the hull against ice because, although the hull strakes are three-centimetres teak, I had no wish to see them threatened. The suggestion was put forward that we sheath the whole hull with aluminium or stainless steel sheet, but I was nervous of this and in the end we carried large timbers on board which were strapped either side of the bow to push through the ice. It may seem slightly absurd to have worried about landing people and gear from a yacht no larger than a ship's lifeboat but, unlike a lifeboat, *Suhaili* has a draught of a metre and a half. So the expedition was very lucky to be given an inflatable dinghy, plus an outboard engine capable of keeping pace with *Suhaili* for filming purposes, as few people can row at five knots.

Only two things keep me awake at night – an insecure anchorage and the fear of losing all power, so I cannot communicate with the outside world or start the engine. *Suhaili* now possessed a reliable engine with a powerful alternator, but a short in a circuit would drain the batteries and I wanted a backup battery-charging system. In the end I had two systems and slept soundly. A wind generator was installed on the mizzen mast and a special solar panel was fitted on deck. The latter also served as a mobile charger for the portable HF set carried by the climbers which allowed regular communication with the boat and Portishead radio when conditions permitted.

Quite where all the crew and equipment were to fit, I had no idea. The main team was five, plus John Dunn from BBC Radio 2 who had accepted an invitation to accompany us until Reykjavik, Iceland's capital. *Suhaili* has six berths, but as Chris relayed the lists of equipment, I realised the fo'c'sle, which contains two of the berths, would be full of sledges, skis and climbing gear. There was no alternative but to adopt the hot bunk system whereby, since two people would always be on watch, the four remaining bunks would be enough for those off duty. Personal gear was to be stowed in bags which, if nothing else, encouraged everyone to be parsimonious with luggage and ensured tidy stowage. At the beginning of June we were just about ready and *Suhaili* was moved to the Joint Services base at Gosport for an engine service. We departed for Whitehaven in Cumbria on 13th July to collect Chris and Jim Lowther, plus all the land equipment and food. From Whitehaven we planned to sail to

Reykjavik, drop off John Dunn, pick up a two-man film crew, review the ice situation and then head for Greenland.

Whitehaven was frantic for the crew. For a start, we had developed a leak in the vicinity of the sternpost and were taking in water quite rapidly. My worst fear was that a hull plank had sprung, but when we dried out alongside Britain's last serviceable steam dredger, we were much relieved to discover it was due to an old electric cable trunking for an echo-sounder inserted when she was built. The hole was quickly plugged, but not before it caused a certain amount of alarm amongst the climbers. Two months' stores for six people occupied all the locker space and when the fo'c'sle was loaded with six sledges, a dinghy, petrol cans and all the remaining gear, it was almost full. The consolation was that whatever weather we encountered, it would be hard for anything to shift! *Suhaili* had sunk by ten centimetres at this stage, indicating a cargo of two tons in total, but we hoped this represented all our requirements. At 1800 on 19th July we motored out from the harbour with almost half the town to see us off – our adventure had begun.

2 Whitehaven, Rockall, Reykjavik

The light wind died once we cleared the sloppy waves around the harbour, so we proceeded steadily under motor. Every half hour Perry and I, like small boys with a new toy, used this as an excuse to poke our noses into the engine compartment and check the gleaming new machine. We set sail as well because the initial pitching motion had turned some of the crew a little green and I thought activity would distract their minds from queasiness and provide a steadying effect on the boat.

Seasickness expresses itself in many forms from outright illness to feeling slightly tired and, apart from pills, the only cures are activity and time. The crew sat around the cockpit, the newcomers looking rather apprehensive, perhaps thinking that if the sea was so uncomfortable with land still in sight, what lay in store further out? Departures are always bitter-sweet occasions. One part of you is excited at setting out on a new adventure, the other is sad at leaving friends and loved ones. However, it felt good to be back on a moving boat with a distant objective and the prospect of sampling a new sport. In the meantime there was a crew to organise.

In the rush to load everything at Whitehaven there was no chance to instruct the newcomers so, once we were underway, we went through the names and functions of the boat's parts which they must learn. We then explained the drill for various emergencies, such as man overboard, and the most important lesson of all, 'have one hand for the boat, but always keep one for yourself', because if everyone remembers this, that particular emergency should not arise. I set the watches with the idea of balancing experience; John Dunn and myself, Perry with Chris, James and Jim (the latter was christened the James watch or Young Turks, since they were the youngest and the most energetic). It would have been nice for Chris and me to be together, but I thought he might find it easier with a third party and as John had the least sea time, it seemed sensible to pair with him. This system also allowed the team to become well acquainted. We could always swap around later if everyone's topics of conversation were exhausted. There were almost a thousand miles to Reykjavik and if the wind came on the nose, the passage might easily last two weeks.

We motored steadily towards the Mull of Galloway, rounding it into a foul tide at 0315 the following morning and we passed the Mull of Kintyre ten hours later. Now there was a choice of courses, we could go up the Sound of

Jura and inside Mull and the Hebrides, or west into the Atlantic. The wind was from the south, still too light to push us at more than two knots, but at least it was favourable and knowing how badly *Suhaili* sails to windward, I felt it advisable to make as much westing as possible. The prevailing winds are from the west and a southwesterly would be fine for Iceland, but if a depression came through and the wind veered northwest, we would be stopped dead. Anyone who listens to the shipping forecasts knows depressions always seem to head for Iceland – it attracts them like a magnet. So the course was set to pass Islay into the Atlantic, but not before James and Jim and I had jumped overside for a swim, a habit I encourage at the beginning of a voyage, as salt water keeps the body fresh. I have to say the water was not warm. We continued under motor in order to make good progress and could have connected the Autohelm and been very idle, but the calm weather not only allowed everyone to settle in and adjust to the routine, but also learn to steer.

At first sight steering by compass appears a simple affair, but it usually takes time for anyone to understand the principle that the boat is moving not the compass card, and there is a tendency to put the helm the wrong way, paying attention to the compass the whole time, not to the sea and the feeling of the wind. Happily, the newcomers sorted this out quite soon and we progressed to the finer points of steering to the sails. While it would have been easy for the old hands to steer and thus avert risk to the gear, I have always believed the quickest way to learn anything is to do it, and the idea was to turn our landlubbers into seamen. There was no way they would become expert during the expedition, but I aimed to make them efficient about the deck. Luckily *Suhaili* is a tough lady with strong rigging, so she absorbs abuse which would cripple a modern yacht. I soon found John could be left on the helm whilst I adjusted sails or listened to a weather forecast, and Chris and Jim were equally well advanced. It was encouraging to see their assurance grow each day as they discovered sailing is not just a question of sitting back and allowing the sails to propel the boat. There is constant work to do, from trimming sails and navigation, to regular maintenance and feeding, and this goes on around the clock. As my confidence in the crew rose we became more adventurous. On the 24th, although the wind was from the northeast about force 5, I decided to set the huge balloon of the spinnaker, which increases the sail area by 150 per cent. For five hours we held it, averaging over six knots in a glorious broad reach, but when the wind increased slightly I lost my nerve and it was handed with everyone assisting for the practice, and we reverted to plain sail, but not before all the crew had had the opportunity to steer and feel a real pull on the helm from the extra power, and enjoy the sensation of *Suhaili* moving at almost her maximum hull speed.

Chris, who had started the voyage gazing yearningly towards the indistinct but to him desirable sea cliffs of the north-east corner of Ireland, was beginning to get into the nautical spirit of things, as his diary shows:

'Taking the helm is a real learning process. At first I was just clinging to the compass. I'd been told to steer a course of 340° and tried to keep on it. Then Robin or James or Perry would say, well you also need to look at the sails and the sea. I found that very difficult. Difficult to see any pattern in this chaos of waves that seemed to be coming at us in every direction. Then the pattern began to emerge and I also saw what happens when you go off course. We gybed, the sail went smashing across, and Robin explained, not sharply but informatively, that you could actually do quite a lot of damage to the tackle that way and it was something to avoid.

I am impressed by Robin's approach to us landlubbers. He is undoubtedly the skipper and we are undoubtedly going to do what we're told but his way of sharing information, of discussing options, and his own immense knowledge make it an enjoyable education, as I slowly begin to get a feel for the tiller, start to see the waves coming and know to pull it in the right direction so that we don't heel over, and remember to make sure we keep the sails filled. It's physically tiring work because the weight of the tiller in a heavy sea is quite considerable, and it's mentally tiring, too, because as a beginner you're having to concentrate all the time, whereas with Robin and Perry it is clearly second-nature.'

Life evolved into a pleasant routine governed by radio schedules as John reported in to his programme each afternoon. Our entire living accommodation measured only three metres by two, with two bunks set out each side and the floor space limited to a tiny area at the aft end by the galley and chart table. We were so congested that oilskins were removed in the companionway, then carted over piles of gear in the cabin and hung in the loo to drip dry. The small neck towels worn to prevent water entering the collars of the otherwise excellent wet-weather suits, hung from the cabin skylight support, swinging in time to the boat's motion and, apart from not helping those who were still suffering from seasickness, gave the impression we were jammed inside Widow Twankey's laundry. Anyone who popped briefly below had to be selective where they dripped as soaking other people's things was not exactly popular.

Chris and Jim are used to tents and a camp where, whatever the rigours of the day, it is usually possible to have a few moments alone and a good night's sleep. On *Suhaili* they found themselves permanently confined in a space no larger than a tent, and with no privacy at all. The hardest discipline to get used to is probably watch-keeping and a sleep pattern with a maximum of six hours rest and then three hours work. While the jerky, bumpy, rolling and pitching movement, which can catch even a seasoned hand off balance, often results in bruises if lucky, cuts if not. Even the simplest action takes time and patience.

> 'Making tea I got catapulted across the cabin with an open sugar bowl in my hand. Result – sugar everywhere, the cutlery drawer all over the place, and then you've just got to clean it all up, and get on with the job. But I'm enjoying this. I'm sure it's going to stretch me to the limit, but it's what I need.'

Spilling the sugar was the least of our worries and it soon dissolved into the bilges. More of a nuisance, the Weatherfax, which provides the best detailed weather forecasts, had broken down. So we had to rely on the skimpier shipping forecasts that concentrate on the main systems and don't tell you the half you'd like to know in a small boat in sudden force 5 westerlies. Potentially more serious were the antics of the radio which refused to transmit, although it was receiving perfectly well. In the ordinary way this would not have been a disaster as there are many reasons why radio contact is broken and no one at home worries immediately, but John was dependent upon it for the *John Dunn Show,* so it was critical. A kindly giant of a man at six foot seven inches, poor John must have suffered even more than the climbers in accommodating himself to the constrictions below deck. But throughout our efforts to resuscitate his professional lifeline he remained imperturbably calm and never raised his voice. There was not a radio engineer amongst us and, in any case, with modern synthesised sets there is little anyone can do at sea. However we felt we should check for obvious faults, so Perry and I removed the set, cleaned it and then inspected the tuner where we found a loose wire. After a considerable delay spent poring over the manual, this was reconnected and we called Portishead who, much to our delight, responded immediately. Thus encouraged, we turned our attention to another casualty, a constantly leaking WC which had forced us to resort to the old standby 'bucket and chuck it' – perfectly adequate, but not very civilised. The trouble lay with the valves connecting the unit to the sea about a metre below the waterline. However, once the hull valve was removed, Perry cleaned and greased it, while I jammed my hand over the rush of Atlantic into the boat and, when re-assembled, we had a working WC. Twin successes called for a celebration and we declared a 'Headland'.

The 'Headland' policy was developed by my friend Billy King-Harman and me in the 1986 Round Britain Race when we were becalmed in a small bay to the south of Lerwick in the Shetland Isles and could not persuade our large catamaran to tack. As the sea-room diminished, the situation became extremely hazardous and eventually we attempted to wear round (turning the boat away from the wind) to achieve the opposite tack. We were perilously close to the cliffs but round she came and, as we sheeted in the sails to beat out into clear water, we looked at each other in relief and promised ourselves a nip of whisky when we passed the headland which marked the bay's limits. The toasting of headlands became a tradition thereafter, the rule being that when the skipper and crew agree a headland is passed, out comes the whisky. The rule is modified once there are more than two people on board, and I democratically allow three votes – the skipper has one, the crew collectively another, and as owner I have the casting vote. It works well in practice and I cannot recall any disputes! We soon had another excuse for a Headland when we received news that John Dunn was a grandfather. A bottle of champagne had been hidden away in expectation of the event and we well and truly wetted the baby's head.

James, Perry and I kept one secret from the mountaineers. As we had charge of navigation there was no reason why they should discover we were edging a little further into the Atlantic than was strictly necessary and heading for what we kept referring to as way point R. What we knew and they didn't was that way point R is Rockall. None of us had seen this isolated rock hundreds of miles from anywhere which was only claimed by Britain during my lifetime. Inexorably our course closed in and it was sighted in poor visibility at 0720 on the morning of 24th July. Just over an hour later we sailed to within thirty metres of the surprisingly small outcrop, about the size of an average house. There was very little guano on it, probably because winter waves sweep right over it and deter nesting. It was a great disappointment that the wind was force 5 from the west by north and the swell consequently far too heavy to risk a landing with the dinghy, so we approached as close as we dared and left the landing for another occasion. Apart from providing a pleasant talking point, this also enabled us to check the accuracy of the GPS which seemed to be giving a position to within six metres.

The GPS, or Global Positioning System, is quite remarkable. Its very recent use in the Gulf War is widely known, but the civilian version is supposed to have a degraded performance and be accurate to within thirty metres. It had appeared more precise when tested in Whitehaven and the latest check was equally encouraging. We made some further experiments using the sextant, mainly because I wanted Perry to revise the old-fashioned methods and James to understand them. In fact James's navigation was advancing in leaps and bounds. His first attempt at a meridian altitude was eighty miles adrift, but as we progressed towards Iceland the results improved dramatically. The crunch came when I was challenged to produce one. I went below after measuring the noon altitude of the sun, hoping for a quick glance at the GPS, but Jim's hand was placed firmly over the screen. I calculated the figures carefully and, to my relief, the difference with the GPS was three cables or 0.3 of a nautical mile. I was secretly rather pleased but resolved not to take unnecessary risks with my reputation in this way again!

By passing Rockall early in the morning we missed the opportunity to declare a Headland. Instead we deferred it until later in the day when it merged with Happy Hour, a time somewhere between five and six in the evening when everyone gathered together and enjoyed a drink. Often it led to a communal effort in creating the day's main meal, regardless of who was officially in charge, but the 'supervisor' took the credit if the results were good. My forte is stew with lashings of garlic, or a curry done in the pressure cooker. Chris also prides himself on his curries. We had one after James and I had been sorting out another crisis. Trying to tighten the stern gland, James had accidentally sheared off its stud. The stern gland is designed to allow the propeller shaft to turn, but if it works loose, it lets in water and slowly floods the engine room.

Fortunately, I could lay hands on a screw that would fit the stud hole until we got to Iceland, provoking the following observations from Chris:

> 'One of the features, as far as I can see, of life on a boat is that things are always going wrong. I suppose because of the sheer wear and tear of continuous heavy usage in a hostile, corrosive atmosphere. Anyway, Robin just spent an hour upside down in the engine room covered in grease and fixed things. Yet another example of the constant ingenuity that is an essential skill for the long-distance sailor.
>
> One of the most noticeable contrasts between climbing and sailing is in the weather patterns. It seems to change much more quickly at sea than it does even in the mountains, so that one hour there can be rainy squalls and you're wrapped up in your oilskins just two people on deck, and then the sun comes out and it's absolutely lovely. At the moment we've got our sleeping bags draped over the deckhouse, James is reading a book and John Dunn is at the tiller, looking like a hoary old man of the sea, and there's a lovely sense of relaxation.'

Our relaxed voyage was in for a major disruption when I tuned in to the United States Coastguard's weather forecast that evening. Although we were east of their area, they did at least warn of systems heading our way, information which the British forecast does not always provide. Further out in the Atlantic a depression of 982 millibars was moving towards south-east Iceland. There was no possibility of avoiding this, so it seemed best to press on and be ready to heave-to if necessary. I mulled over the situation while taking a turn at the helm. The last thing I wished was to fill everyone with apprehension and *Suhaili* is more than capable of withstanding a gale, but it might be an unpleasant baptism for some of the crew. I could not help recalling the last occasion when *Suhaili* and I awaited a gale or storm with a new crew and ended up dismasted in mid-Atlantic. Anticipating a storm, when you know it is inescapable, is rather like being in a condemned cell. From time to time I popped up to check the barometer or put my head out of the hatch to look at the sky as the wind gradually rose to force 7. The long Atlantic swell was rising and under only jib and fully reefed mizzen, we were bowling along on a broad reach. I was watching for the moment to heave-to and was thankful that Perry and I had constructed two large reels which were suspended from the deckhead in the fo'c'sle and held 100 metres of heavy warp which could be hastily run out astern. As it happened we were lucky, the wind eased in the early hours and was a moderate southerly by daybreak, although the barometer failed to rise until mid-afternoon which kept me in suspense most of the day.

Deprived of the drama of a fully fledged gale, Chris proceeded to create his own minor disaster:

> 'I was chopping onions for a curry in the hatchway and turned to speak to Perry just as the boat rolled and the knife cut a deep slice into my hand. No pain but it was deep. Jim said he had some sutures in his climbing kit and volunteered to stitch me together again. I must say I didn't like the idea of that, but it seemed to make sense to get it healed quickly. So he got out his kit, dripped some local anaesthetic on to the wound, and there was little more than a tiny prick. I didn't have to be at all brave, and was soon enjoying an excellent curry washed down by vodka and tonic. And now I'm on the 9.00 to midnight watch, sitting out in front. I must say Perry's an excellent mentor. He was in the Merchant Navy for four years. He's got a deep knowledge of the sea and like Robin has this wonderful practicality of being able to turn his hand to almost any kind of mending. He's also got a lovely twinkly sense of humour.
>
> It's interesting the different kind of personalities on board. Robin's got tremendous positive drive. To him there's absolutely no question about us getting into Kangerdlugssuaq and him getting up the mountain and when Jim said, "Well, if we get into Kangerdlugssuaq", Robin very firmly said, "There is no if, we're going to get there." I think that's the right attitude because it's that positive drive, tempered with a very proper caution and sense, that has allowed Robin to achieve all the things he has

done. It's fascinating the thoroughness with which he prepared, for instance, for the storm yesterday, insisting that lifelines were out, that everyone clipped on to a lifeline before leaving the cockpit, giving us all another quick briefing about being washed overboard, and the promise, and by golly he does mean it, "We'll come back for you, we'll never leave you behind." It's this combination of thoroughness with positiveness which has kept him alive through a series of adventures and has given him an extraordinary success rate as well.'

I think we all recognised that if Chris's hand failed to heal properly he would be crippled when it came to climbing and this simple accident might well mean the early abandonment of our mountaineering plans. Fortunately Jim proved as adept at suturing as he was at most things, and the cut appeared tidy and clean before he added a robust bandage for protection. Chris, who looked a bit pale while the stitches were inserted, was remarkably unconcerned once Jim had finished.

The strong winds resulted in good day's runs on the 26th and 27th and we averaged over five knots. We crossed the sixtieth parallel on the 26th, a Headland naturally, and were then less than 100 miles away from the nearest part of Iceland, although over 200 miles from Reykjavik. The nights were now so short that even at midnight it was no darker than a reasonable twilight. We were making a very good course towards our way point two miles off Cape Reykjanes, the south-westernmost point of Iceland. There is a line of islands stretching fifty miles south-west from Reykjanes which would require a wide berth if the weather closed in or bad weather was threatened, but since I had huge faith in the GPS and the forecasts were promising, I set a course to pass through the way point.

The first sign of land was puffins, those comical birds who look as though their mothers have neglected to teach them to fly properly. The atmosphere was much cleaner and there were spectacular displays of cloud which gave me concern, but I need not have worried, there were no depressions coming our way. Land showed up at a great range and slowly we identified the cone shape of a volcano. The *Admiralty Pilot* warns of strong currents off Cape Reykjanes and it is not wrong. We were level with Elday Island by dinner on the 28th and had to navigate cautiously to avoid banks surrounded by fierce overflows. The island is a large stack, about 225 metres in height, and prompted Chris into fascinating reminiscences of stacks he had climbed off the north-west coast of Scotland and the Isle of Hoy. In truth I think the climbers were relieved to see land, and I was gratified when they did not doubt its identity!

We ran up the coast about two miles off to see what Iceland was like. The buildings were much the same as along a Scottish coastline, but the land was a moonscape. We lacked a large scale chart of Reykjavik harbour, so approached cautiously and radioed for permission to enter. This was speedily granted and we were advised to proceed to a small marina used by day fishing boats, where we secured. The scenery and atmosphere may vary from port to port, but officialdom is the same worldwide. We waited two and a half hours before an immaculate Customs Officer appeared to give us clearance, by which time the boat was festooned with wet-weather gear and below it looked as if a bomb had exploded. He wrinkled his nose as he inspected our papers and appeared amazed at the quantity of liquor to be bonded. There was no locker which suited his requirements for a safe and sealable store, so we stowed the lot in the WC compartment and he sealed that, although expressing some concern as to how we would manage. It is still unclear whether he was more concerned about our bowels or our livers, but we had no intention of using the WC while in Reykjavik. We had reached port and were off ashore.

It is easy to be slightly euphoric on arrival at a foreign port, particularly one you have not previously visited. However, it had been an extremely enjoyable nine days' trip. We had not after all encountered a gale, but no one was complaining on that score. Nevertheless we had undergone fairly unpleasant conditions and come through them well, I had great faith in the crew who, more to the point, now regarded themselves as *Suhaili's* crew.

3 Arctic Waters

Anyone in doubt about Iceland's major industry needs only glance at the port of Reykjavik to find the answer, packed as it is with fishing vessels of every description, including four whale-catchers moored in the inner harbour. The sharp lines and functionally sleek appearance could only draw admiration from any seaman. They are what they seem, perfectly designed for hunting at sea, but one hopes their working days are over.

Allen Jewhurst and Jan Pester, the camera team, who had flown out from the UK, were already waiting for us and had booked an apartment for the expedition. My first priority was to ascertain the latest ice situation and have the Weatherfax repaired, so while I went searching for the Met Office, Perry and James cleaned out *Suhaili*, and Chris, Jim and John removed all the dirty clothes to the apartment and made arrangements for laundry and meals.

I had envisaged a small town similar to those in northern Norway, but Reykjavik is distributed over a substantial area and consists mainly of smart modern buildings. I was taken to the meteorological station by the Perkins' agents who, finding the engine in good order and having produced a replacement stud for the stern gland, had some time to spare. The ice information was pretty limited because recently the skies over the Denmark Strait had been cloudy, but although fog concealed the bulk of Greenland's coastline, icebergs had been spotted in increasing density at the edge of the fog bank lying thirty miles from the shore. However, the good news was that throughout the previous week the pack ice appeared to be shifting north towards Scoresby Sound and, although no one was certain of the present position, it seemed unlikely that it would return to the south at this time of year. The prospect of fog was very unattractive, but the winds were light and forecast to remain that way, so if we encountered bergs in poor visibility there would not be the added danger of heavy seas. Overall, the signs were as good as could be expected for this region, and since it would take three days to reach the fog bank, when it might have evaporated anyway, there seemed little reason for delay. Once we were ready, the sensible course was to head out in the direction of Kangerdlugssuaq and make decisions on the spot rather than worrying about theoretical pitfalls.

It was now time for us to say goodbye to John Dunn who was returning to London at this point. We all enjoyed a farewell dinner at a fish restaurant with roast puffin on the menu, which was noted but not sampled by our intrepid band. John had become such an integral part of our team that it seemed a shame he had to leave. But the BBC expected him back and umpteen million listeners' gain was our loss.

Next day I located an agent who identified what was wrong with the Weatherfax, but the price of repairing it in expensive Iceland was more than the machine cost when new, so I decided we would continue to manage as well as we could without. Our main problem now was how to transport seven people to Greenland in a boat equipped for six. We could have crushed everyone in, but as we lacked sufficient safety equipment, it was arranged for Allen to fly in on an aircraft chartered by mineral prospectors. The logistics were a nightmare. Allen had to depart from Reykjavik before us, otherwise he faced at least a week's delay before the next flight. There was no accommodation at the glacier employed as a landing strip, so he needed camping gear and food for a minimum of a week, since I could not be precise about our arrival date. We gave him the portable Eddystone radio, worked out a schedule for communicating as we approached the coast, and wondered who would undergo the more dramas before we met again.

For the second and last night in Reykjavik our landlady, Asdis Helgadottir, kindly offered to cook a traditional Icelandic lamb dish. I think we anticipated a leg or chops but what eventually appeared was the best part of a whole animal, beautifully roasted, that had been reared on the family farm. An additional boost for morale was the laundering of every item in our wardrobes, so when we sailed shortly after noon on 31st July we felt wonderfully well fed and clean.

The entrance to Kangerdlugssuaq Fjord lies about 340 miles north-west of Reykjavik across the Denmark Strait. A nice force 5 westerly was awaiting as we emerged from the harbour but this rapidly declined to force 1 or 2 and veered to the north-west with limited visibility. We handed the sails and motored for the rest of the day, with everyone falling back quickly into the watchkeeping routine and Jan replacing John as my watchmate. Now Chris had got the hang of the helm he wanted to start playing with my navigation calculator. Should I be looking out for a crew takeover bid, I wondered? Calms before dawn the next morning heralded a change in wind direction to the north, but it stayed light and we continued our slow plod. It was easy to imagine the giant battleship *Bismarck* racing through these foggy waters in May 1941 en route to her engagement with the *Hood*, shadowed by the cruiser *Suffolk*. The ice then had extended halfway across the Denmark Strait from Greenland.

Perry and I were faced with a messy predicament that morning when we discovered the engine bilge filling with diesel fuel. The source was traced to a leak on a corner of the starboard tank and we spent until noon debating how to plug it and recover the lost fuel, but our attention was distracted for a while by the appearance of two killer whales cruising northwards. Although there are numerous reports of attacks on small boats by these creatures, I have never felt threatened and nothing in their behaviour changed my views on this occasion. During the late afternoon we called the mineral exploration camp near Kangerdlugssuaq and learned that Allen had arrived safely. They told us that they hoped to have a helicopter in the air the next day, and that Allen planned to reconnoitre the Cathedral and view the ice conditions within the fjords. Looking at our present progress and assuming the wind was unlikely to rise or ice block our route and cause delays, I asked them to give Allen our ETA as two days ahead.

We were now well and truly into twenty-four-hour daylight, the sea was very placid and we seemed to be free of the thin mist which relieved me of the worry of not seeing ice. I estimated we crossed the Arctic Circle at about 0830 on 2nd August and as this was far too early to celebrate a Headland, we had a special fry-up for breakfast instead. Jan introduced us to a Scottish dish called skirlie which consisted of fried onions and oatmeal, sprinkled with lots of pepper. Topped with a couple of eggs it was delicious. As if someone had deliberately plotted the theatricals, we were just finishing breakfast when there was a shout from the deck that an object was in sight ahead, and there was our first iceberg. It was below the horizon and therefore difficult to assess its size. Also it was slightly to starboard, so we decided to forego a close inspection and press on until one appeared which did not involve a lengthy detour. In fact the berg must have been a real monster as it was three hours before it lay abeam, by which time we could see mountain tops to the north. As land was at least eighty miles away in that direction and therefore the mountains were not really in sight, this was our first experience of the remarkable refraction which Scoresby described 170 years ago.

To improve the range of visibility, we retrieved the rope ladder, a bargain at the Beaulieu Boat Jumble, from the stores in the fo'c'sle and hauled it up the mast on a spinnaker halyard. It was sufficiently long to stretch from the deck to the upper spreaders ten metres above sea level. Within two hours another berg was directly ahead and it was agreed we should stop to take photographs of *Suhaili* passing it and, if there was an easy access point, we also intended to land. Throughout the afternoon new mountains showed in the distance and the iceberg loomed ever larger, but it was not until 1700 that we were within two miles. It was enormous, perhaps half a mile long and at least sixty metres high and from afar could have been mistaken for two bergs in close proximity, but now was revealed as two peaks divided by a col. The sides were snowy white and opaque, although there were streaks of clear ice running through the structure. This berg, which must have extended almost to the sea floor beneath us, was too huge to have originated in the pack ice and was a discarded chunk from a great northern glacier slowly drifting southwards with the current and melting along the way. Perched near one of the peaks was an extensive flock of seabirds who flew off as we approached. There was sufficient wind to give *Suhaili* four knots of speed as we reached back and forth, totally over-awed by the size, the only sounds being our way through the water and the lapping of waves against a floating mass whose weight surpassed any man-made creation. None of our passes was particularly close as we were on the downwind side and there was a lot of small ice (bergy bits) strewn off to lee-ward. We were also acutely aware that bergs can roll over suddenly as their buoyancy changes during the melting process. The prudent action was stay at least two cables (400 metres) clear. Nevertheless I felt an irresistible urge to examine the giant at close quarters.

There was no hope of boarding it, the sides were too steep, but between the two peaks there was a small bay, sheltered from the waves. I was not prepared to sail *Suhaili* into this bay, but the dinghy and a couple of crew were more expendable. James and Jan volunteered to accompany me, so the three of us piled aboard. I took along an ice pick, as I thought it would be fun to collect thousand-year-old ice and see how it affected the drinks at Happy Hour. All around were sheer bright white walls of dripping ice and the torrential water pouring off the sides impressed us all. In order to acquire the ice samples it was necessary to brave the waterfall as the berg curved inwards at sea level. James took the controls and in we went. We bounced off a few times, but fortunately the smooth surface offered no threat to the dinghy's rubberised fabric, and eventually I succeeded in gripping with the ice pick. The ice was more unyield-ing than I anticipated and each blow rang up my arm, at the same time pushing the dinghy back under the waterfall. Jan, tucked up in the bow, started to laugh and muttered something about the mad axeman, but I was making headway and was finally rewarded when a large slice broke away and tumbled into the boat. Triumphantly we returned to *Suhaili* and were delighted to see the remaining crew had mastered the finer points of the Headland policy and were already lining up the glasses and vodka!

After our successful encounter with the iceberg, interest focused on the east coast of Greenland which was becoming clearer by the hour. As there was no sign of pack ice, this was likely to be our last night at sea and dinner was a co-operative curry with all the crew contributing their favourite ingredients. Perry and Chris were on the darkest watch, but it was still light enough for them to take photographs and the refraction supplied some wonderful sub-jects. To the north bergs not actually in view suddenly appeared as tall pillars, some growing out of the sea, others floating above, the colours varying as the sun's rays struck them. The effect was magical.

I was naturally concerned about the ice and was pleased when we raised the mineral exploration camp and they confirmed the lack of pack ice, but warned the fjord itself was quite congested and we should expect to be greeted by a string of bergs off the entrance. Meanwhile, Chris's interest was focusing on the less mobile natural masses.

> 'We're about fifteen to twenty miles out now, so the mountains are beginning to assume a real stature. You can pick out the mouth of Kangerdlugssuaq and, looking down the coast, you can see the glaciers which come down to the sea itself and the dark loom of the mountains. Not a single one of these peaks that are on the coastline has, as far as I know, been climbed.'

Next morning it was indeed the bergs which signalled where the entrance to Kangerdlugssuaq lay. It is almost impossible to describe the absolute beauty unfolding around us as we entered Kangerdlugssuaq Fjord where enormous chunks of ice, many times the size of a Harrods or Selfridges, lay still in the peaceful water. Beyond these were hundreds more of various shapes and colours, ranging from pure white to deep blue, green and mauve, and some were mud-streaked where the remnants of glacial soil clung to them. Framing the horizon was a solid ring of light brown mountains which, surprisingly, resembled the jebels in Muscat. But for me the strongest impression in this spectacular scene came from the absolute stillness, silence and crystal clear air. It was quite warm in the direct sunlight on sheltered parts of the deck, but aloft on the ladder, every movement of the boat created a noticeable wind chill. The mountains might recall memories of eastern Arabia, but one was quickly reminded by the cold that we were in the Arctic.

> 'The first time I climbed the rope ladder it was quite scary but now I'm going up easy-peasy, one rung at a time! It's good training for the arms this, climbing high up towards the sun. It's a lovely day. There's high cirrus cloud but plenty of blue sky as well. The sky here in the Arctic is a gentle pale blue. The land is incredibly arid though. The rocks on the immediate shoreline wouldn't be good climbing. They're basalt, very mucky and broken. Once we get inland to the Lemon Mountains it's gneiss which is much better. It's immensely exciting. I feel a wonderful sense of contentment. Having got so far, having managed to get here without being seasick, and having learnt a little bit about sailing.'

We had a big piece of luck when we entered Kangerdlugssuaq Fjord. Allen had met up with a group of geologists from the University of Copenhagen who were studying the Skærgård Intrusion and had set up camp on it, very near the spot at the south-eastern tip of Kraemer Island where I had it in mind to attempt an anchorage. Their supervisor, Professor Kent Brooks from Cumbria, had a small red wooden boat, sheathed in aluminium, which was ideal for ice work and he generously put it at our disposal for ferrying gear and team between *Suhaili* and the inhospitable shoreline. Kent had been coming to this part of east Greenland for the past twenty years, so he was an excellent guide and he directed us through a relatively narrow channel into a large sheltered bay. It was almost perfect – protected on the west, north and east by rocky hills and the southern boundary sealed by islets. Large bergs would ground before they could penetrate very far, only waves from the south-west would affect its still-ness, and the fetch could never exceed ten miles. The only possible danger was from the notoriously fierce local winds, but this would be greatly lessened if the bottom of the bay provided good holding for the anchors. We motored into the furthest corner and let go a heavy fisherman anchor and once it was made fast aboard, I put the engine at full astern. The propeller thrashed, creating a huge wash, but the anchor remained firm. My paranoia regarding anchorages was allayed, at least as far as this particular one was concerned.

It was now the middle of the day and while concocting a good lunch we caught up on Allen's news, cross-examined Kent about conditions and were fascinated by his accounts of the local Inuit. A neighbouring Inuit camp was abandoned at the moment, but about four families were expected on the coastal boat in two weeks' time. While they were away their dogs, a lean husky-type, were marooned on an island to prevent escape and provided with a whale carcass for food. If the boat transporting the returning Inuit was delayed, it was bad luck for the dogs. In winter the animals pull the light east coast sledges across the fjords and pack ice and are occasionally employed for trek-king inland up the glaciers, although the Inuit's principal food is found at sea level. Summers are mainly occupied with seal hunting, but narwhals, polar bear and Arctic fox are also pursued. High-speed power boats are available, but the majority of hunters continue to favour the traditional kayaks made now of fibre glass in the UK. It had been a good season so far and no less than twenty-two bears were shot around the fjord until the pack ice moved north and the bears with it. Kent warned us to be careful when the Inuit returned, as they had a democratic way of assuming anything left outside a hut or tent was communal, and were inclined to help themselves. The word was not to leave the boat unattended for too long.

I had mixed feelings about the missing bears because I had rather hoped to see one, but preferably at a safe distance as they are the largest and most power-ful predator amongst land mammals and their only enemies are armed men and killer whales. There are many stories of people being attacked and they can easily out-run a human. Since they can be so dangerous, the Danish Government insisted we carry firearms and I had brought along my rifle in order to acquire a new hearth rug. In practice it would, of course, only have been used in extremis, and the only offensive weapon we carried on the trek was a pack of mini-flares which we trusted would be sufficient to frighten off any bear who was too curious. The rifle remained with the boat and was never fired in anger.

As Kent's knowledge of the fjords and the ice therein was encyclopaedic, we were keen to have his thoughts on our plans. In his opinion the Courtauld Glacier route was out, a view supported by Allen who had flown in and photographed the Cathedral on the previous day. The ice in the lower part of Kangerdlugssuaq Fjord was not too thick. (It looked pretty thick to me!) But further up, beyond where Watkins Fjord joined, it was really heavy and both were adamant that there was no way a boat could safely infiltrate into this region. I was disappointed as Gino Watkins and *Quest* had managed to reach the north-west corner of the fjord and it would have been interesting to make a detour and follow in their footsteps, but *Quest* was much larger than *Suhaili*. Watkins Fjord was not particularly promising either as, although there were fewer large bergs, the mass of smaller ones if sufficiently tightly packed could easily bar our way. There were two routes to Watkins Fjord, one on the east side of Kraemer Island through the Uttental Sound, the other to the west via Kangerdlugssuaq Fjord. However, as the junction of Uttental Sound and Watkins Fjord was apparently completely sealed off, we had no alternative but to attempt the Kangerdlugssuaq route. If that proved impassable too, we were faced with sailing round to Mikis Fjord, which *Quest* had visited to launch her Tiger Moth. But this would mean a march in of about eight days, instead of the four or five we had anticipated. We decided to give Kangerdlugssuaq a go, and Kent volunteered to come with us. The ice was reasonably scattered for the first seven miles and we had no difficulty dodging the bergs. It was exciting. The loftier bergs blocked the view ahead, but as each passed, a new vista opened up. As we advanced there was a definite increase in bergy bits and the gaps between them narrowed. By the time we were level with the entrance to Watkins Fjord, speed was reduced to a crawl and we were conning from the upper spreaders, using extreme rudder angles and very slow revolutions. For this sort of work a variable pitch propeller would have been ideal. Even with the engine frequently stopped, it was necessary to post ice jousters armed with boat-hooks on either side of the bow to nudge away the small pieces. Some of these were no more than a foot square at the surface, but they were extremely hard and could hole the hull planking if hit at any speed. It was some consolation to realise that Allen and Kent's opinions had been correct about the upper reaches of the Kangerdlugssuaq, because if Watkins looked formidable, the other route was certainly out of the question. It had taken three hours to cover the ten miles to the entrance to Watkins Fjord, and it was another six before we arrived at the Sidegletscher which was only four miles further.

We quickly noted the presence of quite strong currents within the fjord; the ice in the central part drifted steadily seawards, whereas at the sides it was comparatively static. Later we were to learn that when the tide turned the bergs would drift back into the fjord as well. The water's movements created swirls and eddies around the larger bergs, some of which were travelling at a speed of at least a knot, and the force threw us sideways. We soon learned to be alert for the currents and, more importantly, avoid those which diverted us directly towards bergs. Although we were aware of the dangers from rolling bergs, within the fjord it was just impossible to maintain a safe distance from every one, and that particular risk had to be accepted in order to progress. Occasionally the currents did actively assist. When the way ahead was barred by a wall of bergs, we stopped and waited for the stream to shift them and open a small channel, through which we dashed at high speed.

The work was exhilarating and yet tiring. Aloft one rapidly got stiff and cold and there were frequent breaks while the lookout descended for a cup of tea. Happy Hour and Headlands were things of the past. In mid-fjord we were being pushed remorselessly seawards by the current, which persisted to within fifteen metres of the north shore. However, more substantial bergs were grounded before reaching this point and, although we were still faced with complicated small lumps, there was nothing within range which could capsize on to *Suhaili*.

Slowly we edged our way east. I was not thrilled with the situation, but at least we were advancing and my spirits rose as I realised that we would, after all, succeed in reaching the Sidegletscher. At 2130 we were one and a half miles away from a huge moraine which concealed the actual glacier, and an hour later we were off a flat ledge of rock lying at the foot of the valley through which the glacier flowed. This was close enough. We let go the anchor about thirty metres offshore in seven metres of water. The engine was switched off and we were immediately enveloped in an almost eerie silence. Our voices seemed to travel for miles and even low conversational tones sounded intrusive. Then slowly some noises became audible; the crunch as two bergs hit, the occasional rippling of an avalanche, but of the background hum which is ever present in Britain, there was no evidence.

The dinghy was launched and the first party of Chris, Jim and I paddled ashore. The outboard was not used as the quantity of ice around was more than capable of damaging the propeller. The paddling proved more troublesome than expected as the moment one punched at the ice, it was the dinghy that sheered away, while the ice remained stubbornly unmoved. Eventually we grounded on a low shelving piece of rock and Chris scrambled ashore. He set his feet apart rather deliberately and then stamped them; the landsman was back in his element, and what an element. Behind lay the wide valley containing Sidegletscher and the rock gradually rose until it met the moraine deposited by the glacier on its way to the sea. To the east was another long mound of broken rock and earth and this extended right into the fjord.

'We'll set up the camp just there,' said Chris, pointing to a spot about thirty metres inland. The small selection of stores we had brought with us were landed, and the dinghy returned for another load. In the meantime Kent had arrived and it was far easier to employ his boat as a ferry. Out came the sledges or pulks, two tents, skis, ski-sticks, pre-packed rations, water, fuel bottles and all the various boots, ropes, and ironmongery which had lain hidden in the fo'c'sle for three weeks. While Chris, Jim, Allen and Jan organised the camp and Kent wandered off to examine the moraine, Perry, James and I prepared an enormous hot curry for everyone in the now strangely empty boat.

Once the shore party was established the intention was for *Suhaili* to sail back to the anchorage as quickly as possible, but by the time the camp was set up and dinner eaten, it was four in the morning and we were all pretty well exhausted. Apart from the risk of ice damage, I was uneasy in case a high wind sprang up. This had happened to Watkins' 1930 expedition when they were mapping the fjord. The waters, whipped up by the wind, became extremely rough and threatened to swamp their boat. *Suhaili* could not be swamped because she is decked, but the consequences of very mobile ice did not bear thinking about. Fortunately the wind remained light and the sky was not threatening, so I decided to sleep first and depart later in the day, especially as the ice surrounding the boat was only moving sluggishly and the odd bump was not even marking the paintwork. We were up at 0930 and cooked a delicious fry-up, partly because we were famished and partly to supply loads of energy for the day. *Suhaili* had come through the night unscathed, but only three metres away a large boulder almost broke the surface. This hazard had not been observed on the previous evening, but the tide was lower now and Kent explained these boulders are frequently dumped close by the foot of glaciers where the ice meets the sea. The Sidegletscher is in fact much smaller now than sixty years ago and we could see scrape marks sixty to ninety metres above the present surface, while the moraine disappearing into the fjord indicated that at an earlier stage the glacier had extended further out. To support this evidence, our rather out of date maps showed the glacier occupying a much greater area.

We weighed anchor at 1030 and began the long slow passage down the fjord. If anything the ice was denser, but we were becoming more skilled at handling the boat and as the water between the bergs was like a mirror we made good headway. Three hours later, having covered about four miles, we were into Kangerdlugssuaq and an hour after that were going along very well, and entered our anchorage at 1700. It was difficult to believe we had been in Greenland waters for just over a day, but already we were learning about the ice, its characteristics and how to navigate through it. Of course the task was made easier by the almost complete absence of wind, but even when the occasional light breeze did disturb the otherwise calm conditions, it seemed to have no influence upon the movements of the ice. The main effect came from the tidal currents, but they were inconsistent and depended on the individual berg's draught and its relative position within the floe. The baulks of timber we had transported all the way from London had yet to be tested, but we agreed that when we returned to the fjord, we would fix them along the waterline forward. They would not deflect all the bergy bits off the hull, as some extended quite a way sideways below the water, but they would help.

We took *Suhaili* to the innermost end of the bay where a small inlet connected with a valley, halfway up which lay the remnants of a prospecting camp destroyed by an avalanche. We put out the sixty-five-pound CQR anchor which Bob Fisher and I had purchased especially for anchoring off Barra during the Round Britain Race, my lighter thirty-five-pound CQR and the fisherman, then two lines from the stern were made fast to rock pinnacles ashore. Knowing that any katabatic winds would whistle down the valley, and that with greater freeboard forward and extra windage *Suhaili* would prefer to lie down wind, the two shore lines were led from the stern so that it pointed into this direction. When we had finished, *Suhaili* was not going anywhere in a hurry, but all the same I was well aware that I was incapable of not worrying about her.

Perry and I made the evening meal while James ferried Kent back to his camp. He had very generously lent us his boat for the return passage to the climbers' camp which we hoped would more than halve the time and be safer than the rubber dinghy. Before leaving we toured the bay, already christened Suhaili Bugt, discussed obvious places for triangulation for the survey which Perry and James were to undertake, and identified a good vertical rock for a tide gauge. Finally I went through the procedures for using the rifle which I was leaving with the boat in case a bear unexpectedly came around, and then it was time for me to leave *Suhaili*. I felt disloyal and wondered why I wanted to go mountaineering anyway. I would have been just as happy quietly exploring the surrounding coastline for two weeks with the small team of sailors. I was also conscious of my responsibilities to my two young friends. But it was too late for a change of heart, and with *Suhaili* out of sight, I would be lying to say she was out of mind, I began to feel excitement and curiosity at what lay in store.

For a change we went via the southern end of Watkins Fjord. Kent's boat was marvellous. With the protected hull we barged through the ice relatively confidently and made excellent speed, halting once to inspect a flat slab of sea ice. Having secured the boat to an outcrop, we walked around it. In its centre was a large pool of icy but fresh water. In fact the water temperature in the fjord was about 1°C and was quite drinkable, with only a slight taste of salt.

We arrived off the camp after a journey of only four hours, less than half the time required to travel the same distance with *Suhaili*, and after a quick cup of tea, and arranging a radio schedule for the next morning, Perry and James departed. I watched them getting smaller as they manoeuvred along the fjord's northern shore until they finally disappeared behind a berg. I had great faith in them but continued to worry, which would not do. They were on their own now and I had a forty-mile trek and a mountain climb to contemplate.

4   Inland to the Mountain

The water was a greenish black in the Arctic twilight, lumps of ice gleaming, slowly rotating and shifting with the current. The shore, our landfall on Greenland, was only fifty metres away. A rocky shelf reached down into the fjord. Behind it lay boiler plate slabs littered with the rocky debris deposited by the receding glacier and beyond the sweep of a scree-clad hill concealed the higher mountains. We'd arrived at last, and even though I was tired from the long day tilting with the ice, I had a feeling of delicious anticipation of the adventure ahead, a sense of homecoming to an environment that was both mysterious and familiar. We'd piled all the land gear – pulks, skis, climbing gear and plastic bags full of hill food – into Kent's boat and he motored it on to the natural rock jetty. It was a wonderful feeling to leap on to solid rock and scramble up the shore of Greenland.

An hour later we had the supplies stacked, a couple of tents pitched and the Primus stove roaring away for our first brew on land. It was very noticeable that the three sailors were all too happy to sleep on board *Suhaili,* while Jim and I, with Allen and Jan, were delighted to be on terra firma. We all slept well that night, and next morning, after a mountain rations breakfast of porridge with masses of margarine and honey, we started sorting our gear into loads as *Suhaili* got under way for her safe anchorage and had soon merged into the chaotic mass of icebergs, with only her masts visible.

We couldn't start pulking straight away as, although there were drifts of old snow all the way down to the sea, there was not enough for sledging. So we were going to have to ferry our loads up the side of the glacier to a point where we could start hauling. I packed my load, strapped the pulk and skis to the rucksack, and heaved up. It probably weighed about twenty-five kilos, which is what a porter will carry in Nepal or Pakistan, but it was desperately unwieldy and top heavy. None-the-less it was a delight to put one foot in front of the other, to be relieved of the confines of the boat and to wonder what lay round the next corner.

Jim quickly pulled ahead round a little bay to the side of the moraine ridge reaching out into the fjord. I decided to adopt my own pace. At first it was easy going over gravel and fine sand that led into a narrow valley between the moraine ridge and the hillside. The first impression was one of a bleak beauty, of rocks in greys and blacks and browns and patches of snow under a grey canopy of cloud. But focusing more closely on the ground I was crossing, I could see signs of colour in the form of a creeping plant growing on the lee side of boulders. There was the Arctic willow, the closest approach to a tree in this part of Greenland, standing nowhere more than a few centimetres from the ground, delicate leaves clinging to thin, tentacle branches. There were mosses, in every hue of green from emerald to dark jade, along the banks of the stream or around seepages in the hillside, and among the moraine rocks were little clusters of pink saxifrage.

The others had waited for me on the crest of the moraine ridge. We were about thirty metres above sea-level. There was no wind and yet the ice in the fjord, driven by invisible currents and tides, was in constant movement, great ocean liners of ice, cruising along, with the smaller flotsam and jetsam crammed around them like so many tugs. On the other side of the fjord was the rounded hump of the hill dominating Kraemer Island, and somewhere tucked away behind it, was *Suhaili's* anchorage.

I kept plodding on. I'm slow, but like the tortoise in Aesop's fable, I don't like stopping and very often get to the end of a journey ahead of the hares. We were now in a desolation of piled rocks, the dirty grey surface of the bare glacier visible ahead. A roar of rushing water and we were faced with a stream in spate. I followed its course until I found a spot where I could leap precariously across. By this time we had all become separated, scattered in the immensity of the boulder-strewn wasteland. I trudged on, picking my way across slopes of rubble, dropping down into another valley between the moraine and the slope itself. The walls of the valley were now closing in, soaring faces of sculpted granite that would give a wealth of rock climbs to anyone with the time to explore them. These peaks were just the outliers, little more than 1,000 metres in height, and yet the rock available represented more than that of the entire Mer de Glace above Chamonix – unnamed, unexplored, unvisited. I stumbled on some tracks and, guessing they must be those of the Lowther Racer, I followed them to a pile of boulders by the side of the glacier where Jim had dumped his load.

'This should do,' he said. 'It's flat enough to start hauling here.' We were just eighty-five metres above sea-level and some two and a half miles inland. It had taken us about an hour and a half to reach, so was a reasonable distance for ferrying our heavy loads. Allen and Jan were just behind me and all four of us, well pleased with our first foray, returned to the shore, picking out a better line for our next trip. It was only early afternoon when we got back. After making a brew and lazing in our sleeping bags, Jim, ever-energetic, announced that he'd do another carry. I was very tired from our first effort, short though it had been, and snuggled deeper in my sleeping bag with my book.

Jim bounded into the camp in the early evening after his second carry and I was starting to cook supper, when Perry and James brought Robin back, bouncing through the ice in Kent's aluminium-plated boat. They joined us for a quick cup of tea before returning to *Suhaili*. Our little land team was now complete.

Robin's introduction to land travel next morning was particularly brutal as he had his pulk to carry up to the dump. I kept close to him to encourage and advise on the easiest line. The round trip took us about three hours and on our return Robin, tired though he was, immediately began setting up our HF radio, so that we could try to communicate with *Suhaili*. This was to be vital for his peace of mind and, more practically, so that we could call them in to pick us up at the end of our climb. The high frequency signal was bounced off the ionosphere so that the mountains between us and *Suhaili* would not impede it, as they would with a VHF transmitter. Perry came up loud and clear on schedule and then to our delight, Robin also got through to Portishead, was patched through to the BBC and brought John Dunn up to date.

We were determined to finish our ferrying operation that afternoon and establish ourselves on the glacier at the site of our dump. Once we had had some lunch we took down the tents and packed away everything that was left. Inevitably, there proved to be more than we had realised and the loads were monstrous, at least thirty kilos each, and the heaviest that I had carried for a very long time. We took with us a small tape recorder for our tape diary, and Robin brought himself up to date on this second carry.

'I think it's 5th August and I suppose I'm somewhere about a hundred metres above sea-level – hard to say. I had my first night sharing a tent with Jim and Chris and today the torture started. Only a couple of miles. Full of enthusiasm, I loaded my pack. I see what Chris meant now about not taking any unnecessary personal gear. I did whittle mine down as much as possible and the only debatable item was a bottle of vodka which I have let by as rubbing alcohol. But in addition I've got what they call a pulk which is a fibreglass sledge about two and a half metres long. The chap who builds these things should not go into building racing boats, he makes them far too heavy. Then there's the towing cradle that goes on top of that, then two skis, and I'm using the ski-sticks to support myself. What makes it worse, with all this lot strapped to my back, I'm very top heavy. I'm not used to this sort of work. At sea it is very different. On a boat you can be sitting there for hours on end and have occasional heavy violent bursts of activity, so you build up considerable strength, but it's used in short bursts.

But the view of the fjord from here is spectacular. It's like what you think the North Pole will look like with all these beautiful icebergs. Each one is a thing of beauty with a lovely variety of colours, shapes and occasionally excitement as one collapses or rolls over. You can spot the ones that have just rolled as they're very smooth on top. There was one that must have been a good thirty metres high, so there's 200-250 metres of it below the surface. It's hard to remember these fjords are incredibly deep. In fact Kangerdlugssuaq is almost 900 metres deep. That's over twice the depth of the Denmark Strait.

Oh boy, I've just realised there's another blinking valley to go through before we rise up again. I don't know which I dislike more. Going down gravity's on your side but it's an awfully unstable feeling with this weight on your back, especially when you know you could topple over head first if you lean forward. I'm assured (although I'm not sure how much I believe these climbers) that tomorrow will be easier. We're going to pull sledges. I'm not all that convinced. I've a nasty feeling that's going to turn out to be a bit of a struggle. And, of course, it'll still be using my weakest part, my legs.

The most impressive thing today is the glacier, though it's disappointing how dirty it is. I never expected that. Our camp is just above the snow line. There were a few crevasses en route and Chris enjoyed telling me a story about a guy who got jammed down a crevasse, they could just reach his hand, and it took him three days to die. Now I didn't tell him any nasty stories of people dying at sea. Why's he done that to me?'

We put up our tents in the late evening and I was heartily glad it was Jim's turn to cook that night. I was as tired as Robin, but after our standard supper of dehydrated stew and vegetables, I went outside to revel in the paradise of rock on both sides of the valley in which we were camped. There were wonderful great 1,000-metre granite walls that would be an absolute joy to climb on. I was already planning routes for the return journey. What was just as pleasing was the way we had travelled to these mountains, by sail, on foot and on skis. It gave a satisfying symmetry to our adventure which you don't get when you hire a plane with skis and fly at vast expense to somewhere like Antarctica for two weeks. We had also had time to become a very close-knit team out of learning from each other. I felt quite incredibly happy and tomorrow I would be fifty-seven.

We were now going to change to travelling by the twilight of the short Arctic night when the snow would be firmer for skiing and crossing snow bridges over crevasses. This meant we had a complete day for a very welcome rest, apart from a short reconnaissance up the glacier to try to see round the corner.

But distances are deceptive in Greenland and after an hour's walk we were still a long way short of the bend. Robin found it difficult to cope with a day of relative inactivity. He couldn't sleep and felt we should be up and doing something. Jim reckoned it was because on a boat there was always something to do, but climbers go from periods of intense activity to periods of lying on their backs. Mountaineering is a patient game. Arctic travel, Jim pronounced, is something you need a good book for, and he disappeared back into his tent.

My own sense of anti-climax came from a different cause. It was 6th August, my fifty-seventh birthday, and no one had said a thing. I sat in the tent trying to read, little tendrils of homesickness nagging at me, when there was a throat-clearing and some laughter outside, followed by a very discordant rendering of 'Happy Birthday to you', and there was Allen holding a miniature bottle of champagne in one hand and a tiny iced cake with four spluttering candles in the other. Apparently it was Wendy who had put them up to it. I was pleased and immensely touched. I tried to blow out the candles, without success as they were the ever-burn variety, shared out the cake into five little morsels, and gave us each a small swig of champagne.

It was 10.30 that evening when we started taking the tents down and packing the pulks. The sun was only just setting, bathing the rounded hump of Kraemer Island in a rich pink glow that soon deepened to purple. There was no point in using skis on the bare ice. Indeed it was so slippery that Jim recommended crampons. I harnessed myself into the pulk which resembled a large version of a children's plastic sledge, with two long strips for runners screwed into the base. A pair of alloy handles, in lieu of traces, are fastened to the pulk and clip into a nylon webbing chest and waist harness for hauling. Ours must have held about a hundred kilos each.

With a ski-stick in either hand, I gave an experimental heave. The pulk slid along the ice amazingly easily, when not jamming against one of the many flutings that criss-crossed the glacier. But although it was uneven progress, it was still much pleasanter than carrying a load. We were six weeks beyond the summer solstice and the nights were beginning to creep in once again. In June, the sun would never have set, making its twenty-four-hour orbit round the dome of the sky, but now each night lasted that little bit longer and was that little bit darker.

I had dropped into a steady rhythm but was impressed by Robin's progress. He was only just behind Jim, going strongly. An hour went by and we had our first stop for a bar of chocolate. Jim recommended ten minutes' rest in every hour. We were now coming up to the elbow joint of the glacier and could get a glimpse of what it was like round the corner. At last we had reached snow and could put on skis. I had bought some plastic skins from the United States which gave better grip going uphill, and presented less friction than the synthetic fur variety available in Europe.

It was real bliss to be on skis and the pulk slid smoothly over the flat surface of the snow which lay on the glacier ice. Our legs moved rhythmically in that constant sliding motion that represents the joy of Nordic skiing – push, slide, push, slide. Without even trying I found myself out in front picking the route in the dark twilight which now prevailed. The glacier was like a pale road between the black pyramid shapes of peaks, highlighted by the subdued grey of snow and ice slopes or icefalls. I didn't want to break the rhythm, longed to see what was beyond the swell of snow-clad ice before me, and went over the hour before pausing at last. Jim was just behind, Jan and Allen quite a way back, and Robin a tiny dot in the distance.

We waited and even got the Primus stove out and made a brew. It was half an hour before Robin caught up. The last time he had been skiing was twenty years before on his honeymoon at Kandersteg, when his mind had probably been on other things. Nordic skiing, towing a big load, is very different from skiing on piste. By the time Robin arrived we were cold and getting impatient and barely gave him time to take off his boots to examine his chafed heels before we were beginning to get back in harness. It's always rough being the tail-end Charlie.

After another three hours and a couple more rests, the early morning sun was bathing first the peaks and then the glacier itself with a rich, warm yellow light and we called a halt for the day, making our breakfast porridge in our topsy turvy time scheme at ten o'clock in the evening before our second night's travel. It was the gentlest of climbs to the head of Sidegletscher and, slowly, the mountains on the other side of Frederiksborg Glacier and then, below us, the glacier itself came into sight. It was huge, bigger and broader even than the Baltoro Glacier in the Karakoram, a gigantic white motorway into the centre of the mountains. There was a drop of a hundred metres or so sweeping gently down towards the side of the glacier and Jim and I revelled in the freedom of the descent and running with our skis. The only one having trouble was poor Robin. Skiing downhill with a pulk when you don't know how to ski, is not fun!

At first glance it seemed easy going across the glacier but I soon found out about the problems Jim had warned of when I arrived on the banks of a surface stream about a metre and a half wide, and obviously deep and very cold. Finding somewhere to cross quickly forced us off course, but at last we found a spot where a kind of ramp led down towards the surface of the water. Jim took his skis off, hurled them on to the other bank and then, taking a run, shot down the ramp, leapt the river and seemed almost propelled by his pulk up the other side. It was my turn and, with a sinking feeling in the pit of my stomach, I followed suit. It was easier than I had anticipated. Soon we were all over the stream, only to be confronted by another. After three hours slogging, we had only made about a mile of progress in the direction we wanted to go, and the centre of the glacier was a morass of waterlogged snow into which Jim sank up to his thighs. Robin, meantime, was also learning the hard way on his blistering heels.

'We're in the middle of the Frederiksborg Glacier. It feels vast, absolutely vast. It's been a bit of a slog both yesterday and today. Yesterday we tried out just about everything, starting off with crampons and then switching to skis and today starting on skis, then we skied downhill for a bit. It's twenty-three years since I last did that and I fell that many times. We decided we'd go for forty minutes and then have a ten-minute break. The trouble is it's taking me an hour to do their forty minutes and then if I'm going to have a break they're having a rest of half an hour. Which means the likes of Jim Lowther gets all fired up and goes off like a racing Sherpa again, and I just fall so far behind that I lose sight of them altogether in this moonscape of ice.

You get over one bit and you're just getting your balance and the sledge comes up behind you and thumps you. Jim's out there striding away – well so a young man should. They told me I should slide these skis but in this sort of muck it's almost impossible. It's rather like one of the route marches of my youth.

A pinky sun is just beginning to kiss the top of the mountains to the south, a really lovely effect, so it won't be long before it's up. I think there may be a depression out in the Denmark Strait. The clouds would indicate a front. The nice thing here is that they really don't seem to be that ferocious and so the weather isn't really bad.

The good news is that the Cathedral is now in sight and ahead of us, up the glacier, there's a huge wall of crevassed ice which we're going to go round to get up above it. So the plan is to get there and make camp tonight, or today rather. Then I can set up the radio and have a talk to *Suhaili* and try to get through to Portishead again. Something we've not managed to do since we landed. Communications are proving a great source of frustration. So are the skins on my skis which keep coming off with annoying regularity. It's bad design, I think. I'm going to take a knife to the back of these skis today and make a little nick to see if that'll solve the problem.'

It was time to stop. At the head of the glacier we now had a clear view of the Lemon Mountains, a superb range named after the man who looked after Watkins' base camp and radio station on the 1930 British Arctic Air Route expedition. At their right, or eastern end of the range, were two sharp pointed peaks called Mitivagkat, which means breasts. They are well named for they look like those stylised African sculptures of sharp pointed breasts, thrust up into the sky. The left-hand one had been climbed by Stan Woolley's expedition in 1972, the only peak in this huge area to be climbed. The Cathedral itself looked magnificent but also worryingly formidable. It was a wedge of rock embracing a snow slope that reached up to its summit but it was guarded by an array of bristling rocky outlying peaks and it was impossible yet to pick out a route towards the summit.

Jim and I decided we needed a reconnaissance to determine whether to approach from the south side, which would give us the most direct route, or try it from the north. It was at this point that Jim confessed that he had forgotten to bring from *Suhaili* the photocopies of all the photographs. Since I hadn't brought mine either I couldn't really complain, and at this stage it did not seem to matter too much. We decided that we would have a short leg that night, stop at the bottom of the side glacier leading to the south side of the mountains, and then Jim and I would push on by ourselves, travelling light, to make our reconnaissance.

That night we went through a heavily crevassed region, zigzagging from side to side to find a way from one snow bridge to the next, with dark chasms looming on either side. We didn't rope up because Jim said that when hauling a pulk you got into a desperate tangle with the rope on, and anyway, if you did go into a crevasse, there was little anyone could do to stop you going to the bottom, rope or no rope. The peaks of the Lemon Mountains, black against the clear twilit sky, made a dramatic silhouette, reminding me of a fairytale city hiding behind a turreted wall. We stopped at about 3.00 a.m., put up the tents, had a brew, dozed for an hour or so, and then dragged ourselves off for our exploration. I felt tired and unenthusiastic as we set off, but the moment we started gliding over the snows, free from the cumbersome restraint of the pulks, I was filled with a joyous anticipation and well-being. We were in the heart of the mountains, far from any other people, about to try to find a way up the Cathedral.

It took us an hour to get near the head of the glacier. One branch led up to what was either a col, or an upper corrie leading along the southern aspect of the mountain, which seemed to drop in a series of steep rocky buttresses and deep-cut gullies, threatened by seracs, down to the other side of the col. We debated whether we should go up to the col, but eventually opted for getting a more distant perspective from the other branch of the glacier. But the higher we got, and the more we saw, the more dispiriting it appeared. The southern aspect was both complex and formidable. As we skied down the glacier in a series of long exhilarating runs, we agreed that we would have to look at the northern aspect. Surely there must be an easier way up the Cathedral.

We got back to the camp at about ten o'clock in the morning and described our findings to the others while Robin cooked us a magnificent meal. It was only then that we started looking at the map once again and slowly the realisation came that we had perhaps misinterpreted the ground. Looking at the map, the Cathedral, or *Domkirkebjerget* as it is described in Danish, lay between the two branches of the glacier, not on the right of the right-hand branch, as did the peak we had identified as the Cathedral on Stan Woolley's photographs. The peak between the two glacier forks was not as dramatic as the one we had been looking at. It was a great hummock of a mountain with very little snow and a coxcomb of pinnacles on its crest. This was the peak, however, that Allen Jewhurst had flown over when he had his ride in the helicopter. In other words, from a height above the Frederiksborg Glacier it had seemed the dominant peak. We gazed at the map and then up the valley at the two peaks, the one on the left was undoubtedly the Cathedral, according to the map. Point 2,600 metres, which we had perceived to be the Cathedral, was a more attractive peak but the Cathedral, as marked on the map, was the highest point of the Lemon Mountains and had the very real attraction of being readily accessible. We could also see an obvious line up a wide ice gully, leading to a col at the foot of its south ridge, which swept in a series of rocky steps and pinnacles towards the summit. Our schedule was tight. We could only allow a week to find a feasible route on the mountain and then climb it. So we decided to go for the Cathedral as marked on the map, because it seemed to offer a greater chance of success. Early the following morning we pulked up into the cirque immediately below it. Robin describes his impressions in his diary.

> 'I think one of the things that strikes you about this place is the sheer scale of everything. I was looking down the Frederiksborg Glacier the other day and I did a mental calculation – there were 150,000 acres of glacier just there sitting in front of us, and all surrounded by these huge rocks. Now in our little side valley, it's strange to think we're probably the first people to set foot here. In fact we're only the third party to walk up the Frederiksborg Glacier. And it's absolutely beautiful.'

It was indeed an impressive spot, the walls of the Cathedral mass dropping sheer on to the flat head of the glacier nestling in the cirque. There was scope for every style of mountaineering, big wall climbing on the steep granite walls, particularly on the right-hand side of the cirque, Scottish-style winter climbing up deep, ice-filled gullies that followed the basalt fault lines, and a classic ridge by which we hoped to climb the Cathedral.

We planned to start the next day but I was uncomfortably aware at how little Robin knew about climbing. Since our day in the Cuillins ten years ago, he had

had one evening of basic instruction in London, courtesy of the Royal Marines, and one all too brief outing with me on Derbyshire gritstone. I had hoped to run out a few rope-lengths up the gully leading to the foot of the ridge to see what the climbing was like and to show Robin the basic principles of ice climbing and abseiling. The sun crept round to it at about eight o'clock in the morning, however, and a fusillade of stones rattled down the ice. It was not a good place to hold a climbing school. So after we had had a brew, we trailed over to the foot of a gully still in the shade on the other side of the cirque.

It was a pretty intensive lesson. I showed Robin how to put on his harness, checked he knew how to tie a prusik knot, and then I led up a little ice slope which steepened to about seventy degrees at its top. Robin describes the experience.

> 'Did a bit of abseiling, using axes and crampons to get up fairly steep surfaces and Chris also showed me how to brake a fall. After the first time, once you are convinced the system works, it's quite fun that, just letting yourself go down the slope and then braking.'

But through all these strange new experiences he remained very much the skipper of *Suhaili*.

> 'Radio communications have been a bit of a disappointment. We still haven't been able to raise Portishead again, although I've heard aircraft all over the place calling in. I don't suppose we'll get them from here anyway because we're surrounded by mountains. Perry came through very clearly today from the boat and, although he wasn't able to hear me, I could hear him and was able to get some news. James apparently fell in yesterday because he failed to secure the dinghy properly – well either he fell in or had to dive in, because if they lose the dinghy they're a little bit mucked up. They seem in fine fettle. They've obviously been getting on with the survey of that little anchorage I asked them to do and today they said they were going to do soundings, so they'll start building up an underwater profile of the anchorage. This sort of information may not be used that often, because I'm not sure many yachtsmen come up here, but that anchorage did look so protected that I think it's worth recording it and passing the information on in case anyone else needs somewhere nice and safe and sheltered to moor up.
>
> We're having to start to think a little bit now about going back and how we're going to do it, and this involves how much ice

there is in the Watkins Fjord. Can we get the dinghy in there? Kent Brooks has taken his boat round to Mikis Fjord, about twenty miles further away. Our little rubber dinghy isn't honestly totally suited to navigation in heavy ice. And I don't really want Perry and James bringing *Suhaili* round on their own, simply from an insurance point of view. We could go back the way we've come to Watkins Fjord, have a look and dump the gear, then trudge on around to Sdalen. It'd take us about four days, I suppose, and we'd need a helicopter to get the gear out. I don't think any of us likes that option – not the trudge, nor using a helicopter. The alternative is that we talk to Perry in a couple of days, when we finish the climbing, and ask them to nip round and look at the fjord and see if he thinks he can get in.

Chris and Jim are very keen to do another climb but although there may be time for it I think it's something that has to be secondary. We do need to get out of here and this ice in the fjords is something that you cannot predict. There's a bit of cloud scattered above us. Cumulus, nothing too serious. There was a little bit of cirrus yesterday which usually indicates some strong winds but they don't seem to have appeared and, even if they did, I'm not sure whether they'd have much effect in this sheltered place.

Tomorrow's the big day. We'll get up at 4.00 a.m. and go for the slope. It looks like about 300 metres of ice to climb first. It seems an awful lot. We're already at 1,500 metres, which is over 4,600 feet. We're camped in a valley which is higher than the highest mountain in Britain. Now we're talking about another 300 metres of sheer ice. It looks fairly vertical, though Chris thinks it won't be when we get to it, and then across the top it looks a bit of a scrabble. The idea, and it seems sensible to me, is to get up the ice during the dark when it's firm and then have the sun on our backs when we're up the top, where the chill will be that much greater. Well, we'll see. The only thing I can say is that I wish my legs felt stronger. But otherwise I think I'm pretty healthy. This living obviously suits, well humans are meant to work physically, aren't they. And it's good to have a lot of hard work you can't avoid. It forces you to get fit. All the same, I won't be sorry when I don't have to use my legs quite so much. The poor things are suffering a little bit.

One thing I'm missing is decent food. This dehydrated stuff is awful. The other day on the glacier I suddenly felt a craving for a real orange. I must say another good reason for getting back to the boat is so that we can have much better quality of diet. I'm sure it's very nutritious and everything else, but I wouldn't like to be on this stuff for much longer. In fact, I'm beginning to start fantasising about eating. I'm already deciding the meal for when we get back. We'll have a dirty great curry with a choice of sauces as that will be our final meal before we leave Greenland and set out on the voyage home.'

We packed our sacks that afternoon. I was convinced we could complete the climb within the long Arctic day. Jim, after all, had never had to bivouac in all the climbs he had done in Greenland. We were at a height of 1,500 metres which gave us just over 1,100 metres to go to the summit. We therefore didn't bother with any bivouac equipment, we would take a reasonable rack of rock pegs, nuts and Friends, two water bottles each and an ample supply of goodies. We then settled down for the night. I had that sense of excited anticipation, combined with anxiety, that I always have before a big climb but as I snuggled into my sleeping bag I couldn't help worrying about how Robin would cope with the climb ahead.

5   The Cathedral

I'd been awake for some time but didn't want to plunge into the reality of the cold dawn and the effort of the day ahead. It was my turn to cook breakfast. That meant struggling with the kerosene stove. I snuggled deeper into the womb-like security of my sleeping bag, allowing myself five more minutes before I opened the zip and peered out. It was 3.30 a.m. The sun hadn't yet come up and the sky was a washed-out grey, making it difficult to tell at first glance if it was clear or covered in high cloud. But its very clarity showed that it was clear. Another fine day and our chance for the summit.

I soon had the stove purring. There was no sign of movement from Jan and Allen, though I could hear the roar of the stove from their tent. I settled back in the sleeping bag to wait for the water to boil before thrusting mugs of tea, heavily laced with sugar, into the hands of my two partners and we were ready to face the day. Standard breakfast was porridge with honey and margarine.

Jan and Allen were away first. They were only going as far as the foot of the gully to film the start of the climb. Jim was away next, closely followed by Robin. After finishing my cook's chores I caught up with them at the bergschrund, put on the rope and started up the first pitch, running out the rope's full length. It developed into a steady rhythm, front-pointing up the 40° ice, hacking out a stance, putting in an ice screw and then bringing up Robin, while Jim ranged unroped, at first accompanying Robin, giving him advice and encouragement, and then pushing on ahead. It wasn't difficult, but as is so often the case, the scale was much greater than it had looked from a distance. It took us eleven rope-lengths to reach the top. By that time Robin had become confident on his crampon points and had picked up the rope work on the stances remarkably quickly.

> 'It was not until we reached the top of the ice wall that I calculated it was one and a half times as high as the Canary Wharf Tower, some 350-400 metres, according to Chris's wrist barometer. But I felt complete trust in their belay system. Chris inspires confidence. He is obviously so happy and at home in these conditions and at the same time extremely conscientious about safety.

I took a little time to get the hang of high stepping in crampons on the flat. On the ice however, life was far simpler, as the
slope meant that, except when resting at the end of a pitch, only
the toes of the boots were involved. So we went, pitch by pitch,
with left axe, right axe, stretching out upwards as far as comfortable, and then left foot, right foot, making sure they had gripped,
then repeating the whole process.

The ice surface was very hard, but occasionally there were
patches of snow which were easier to manage and the tents and
valley below slowly grew smaller as we rose. At each pitch, once
anchored and having cut a small shelf to rest one's boots, there
was a chance to look around and the view was breathtaking, the
air so clear you could see as far as the sharply outlined horizon.
It gave a great incentive to climb higher just to see further.'

As we neared the top, the sun hit the rocks above us on either side of the gully
and the occasional fusillade of stones came rattling down.

It was 8.30 a.m. when we reached the col and gazed over the other side at a
jumble of craggy peaks, icefalls and tumbled glaciers, all of them untouched,
unexplored. The sun was pleasantly warm and we sat down, had something to
eat and drink and sorted out our gear for the climb ahead. The ridge seemed
an easy scramble with rakes of scree and short rocky steps. I decided therefore
to leave our ice axes and only take one pair of crampons. Coiling most of the
rope and carrying it around my shoulder, I had Robin on a short length,
intending to take him up guide-style, keeping the rope taut at all times so that,
should he slip, I could immediately respond, and heave him back into
balance.

We set off, Jim ranging on ahead to pick out the route, while I followed more
slowly, plodding up the stretches of scree and scrambling up the little rock
walls. There was an occasional awkward step which slowed Robin down. Jim
had gone out of sight and beyond shouting reach. This meant I no longer had
my route-finder and had to start picking out a line for myself. The way led up a
steep little groove with a hand-jam crack at the back. I thrutched up it, took a
good stance to hold Robin and talked him up, trying to explain the principles
of hand jamming. Though we had had some practice a few months earlier on a
gritstone crag in Derbyshire, Robin did not find it easy.

'As we made our way upwards, the climbing seemed to be progressively more difficult. At one point we were faced with what
appeared to me like an impossible vertical face, but after looking
at it for a couple of minutes, Chris found a route and started to
climb. Once he found a ledge he took in the slack on the safety

line and called down for me to follow. I looked up and was alarmed to see the best part of Chris's boots sticking out over a ridiculously small ledge. I did not like to say anything, but it did not look as if he could hold me if I fell and this was certainly the hardest pitch yet. To make matters worse, as I gingerly stepped out and placed my boot on a tiny ledge, no more than a couple of centimetres deep, I realised I was looking down vertically perhaps 900 metres to the mountain's base. I took a deep breath, this was not the moment to wonder what on earth I was doing here. If Chris thought it possible, it probably was all right. I put my weight slowly on to the ledge and searched around with my hands for something to grip.

From above came Chris's voice.

"What are you doing?" I yelled that I was looking for a handhold. "You don't need one, just use your legs," came the far from encouraging response.

"You may not have needed one but I bloody do," I shouted. Chris and other mountaineers might feel secure just relying on their legs, but after a lifetime at sea always making sure of a good handhold, my instincts, when feeling endangered, were to have a firm grip. Fortunately I found a small crack and commenced hauling myself up as I could sense Chris was becoming impatient – which I later recognised as the outward sign of his growing unease.

This climbing was far more strenuous than anything I had tried in the Cuillins, and although I was enjoying considerable satisfaction every time I reached the top of an awkward pitch and felt I was improving, I was still terribly cautious and slow in comparison with the others.'

I saw some boots dangling over a boulder thirty metres above, and yelled to Jim that it would make life a lot easier if we kept together. He had been taking a siesta in the sun and when Robin and I caught up with him we ate some chocolate and had a swig of water before setting out once again. Amazingly, there were signs of life in what at first glance seemed an arid world. Fragile yellow Arctic poppies clung to sheltered corners on some of the ledges, a big bumble bee bustled along in search of nectar and a pair of snow buntings dipped past the ridge. But it was after midday and we still had a long way to go. A grey scum of high cloud had been creeping across the sky, and was now overhead. Jim was sanguine, assuring us that as long as we could see the Watkins Mountains to the north-east it would be some hours before the weather broke. I wasn't so sure. I was getting increasingly worried about the slowness of our progress and our prospects if we had to make an epic retreat in bad weather. Robin was as cheerful as ever but the climbing was becoming more difficult and he was having trouble in following me. I couldn't help expressing my doubts.

'If we don't manage to go any faster and this weather looks any worse, we might have to think of calling it a day.'

'Look, if I'm holding you up, you could always leave me here and press on more quickly,' was Robin's response.

'No. We couldn't possibly do that. We must stick together.'

'I'd be all right. We've got to make it to the top.'

'You'll do as you're told,' I flared. It was a completely unjustified explosion caused by the extent of my concern. I apologised immediately and Robin assured me, as I knew anyway, that he would do exactly as he was told.

I had seen from the bottom that our way to the summit mass was barred by a huge pinnacle which I was hoping to bypass. Looking from the col, there had appeared to be some scree ledges reaching out across the left-hand, or western, face that would enable us to do this, but now, as so often happens, this proved to be an illusion. The easier line led across and up a series of basalt dykes across the right-hand, or easterly, face. We followed these and about four o'clock in the afternoon reached a shoulder below the pinnacle. It was not reassuring.

The pinnacle seemed so much bigger than it had been from the bottom and the drop into the gully, which was the alternative route, avoiding the pinnacle, was both long and steep. I couldn't see the top of the gully as it was hidden by the pinnacle. All I could see was its snow-clad bed and ice-glazed rocks on the walls to either side. We certainly couldn't go that way, since neither Jim nor Robin had crampons. We'd have to go over the pinnacle. The face above the gully seemed to have the easiest line of weakness, but the ledges were covered in snow and the rock was chill in the shadow. I reached a little bay at the foot of the pinnacle, brought Robin over, and started up an open groove in the corner. It was split by a wide crack, reminiscent of gritstone. I was quite tired, and with big double boots and a rucksack on my back, I felt heavy, clumsy and fearful. Even a minor fall and injury would have been desperately serious. I thrutched and struggled, did everything I had been telling Robin not to do, hugged the rock, reached up too far above me, finally managed to place a Friend in the crack above me, straddled clumsily and thrutched up to a ledge from where I could bring up Robin and Jim, who had put on the rope.

We now had two choices, either to continue up the groove line to the left, which seemed to ease, or follow one steeply to the right across the wall above the gully. It was Jim's turn to lead and he fancied the easier looking line to the left, but I was anxious to try to bypass the top of the pinnacle and reach the col behind it, and therefore urged Jim to take the right-hand line. He started up, quickly disappearing round the corner, but from the slowness of the rope running out through my hands and the grunts I could hear from above, it was obviously hard climbing. Here is Jim's view of our activities.

'Up to the base of the pinnacle the climb has been fairly straight-forward, consisting of mixed easy rock and ice climbing with the odd scramble thrown in. Chris led his pitch of severe and I stood at the bottom waiting while Robin followed up. It looked awk-ward with a large flake laid back from the rock, and filled with ice behind. Provided you hung outwards from the flake it was okay, with small thinnish footholds, and Chris had made it look easy. Robin got about halfway up this and started "umm-ing" and "aa-ing" about footholds and handholds and whether there were or weren't any. It had become our standard practice up to this point, and it seemed to work, that I would stand at the bot-tom shouting up to Robin,

"Left a bit, right a bit, there! That's your right foothold . . . now your left foot . . . see if you can stretch up to that wrinkle of rock by the foot of the flake."

At this stage Robin was doing marvellously considering this was his first ever proper climb, and if I'd been in his boots I don't think I'd have kept my cool and patience as long as he had. But he was getting more and more tired, as we all were, and his climbing technique was becoming less efficient. Instead of using his legs to maximum effect, and pushing up on them he was doing the opposite, pulling up on holds with his arms, and of course to keep that up with a sack on your back you need to be something of a Rambo.

I remembered Robin saying something on the boat about only using your legs for balance. On a boat, he explained, arms are what do most of the work. So here he was, on a mountain, doing what his body was used to – using his arms. I knew exactly what he was thinking.

"Oh! I'm going to fall off unless I hang on tighter, and the tighter I hang on the more tired my arms get, so sooner or later I definitely will fall off, unless I get my feet on to something, but the rock's blank, and everybody's shouting about this and that foothold and I can't see any of them!"

At the top of his pitch Chris wasn't quite his normal bubbly self. Robin was just as quiet, and so was I – leaving the leader to his job of leading. Above us the rock looked blank and over-hanging and to the left there looked to be a way up some broken but tricky looking flakes and blocks. Chris thought that the way went up to the right, up a chimney, and then a steep bit to a platform with one more steep bit above that. It was my turn to lead so this was the route we chose. To start with I could hardly fit inside the chimney – it was about the width of my body – and with the rucksack on my back there was a lot of friction coming from the walls on both sides. But with a bit of puffing and panting I squeezed my way up that and then paused to look up at a smooth-ish steep corner with little on offer in the way of holds.

The corner, when I was on it, was delicate and thin, about HVS, and the exposure was terrific because at this point of the climb we were on the face of the mountain. Robin got into some difficulties on this, again because of the leg/arm problem and I was having to give vertical assistance by heaving in on the rope. I was in the middle of a strenuous heave when a cheery "Hi, there" floated down from above. It was Chris peering down, saying how nice the view was and how he'd found a really easy way up to the left, and I'd been right after all.

"Don't worry," he said, "I'm just popping back down to get my sack, and when I'm back up here I'll let down a top rope and bring you both up. This is the top of the pinnacle by the way."

I asked him what it looked like on the other side.

"Well," he replied, "I think we should have gone round the bottom of the pinnacle, so it looks like this is about as far as we're going to go.'"

By the time Robin and Jim were on top of the pinnacle with me it was around 6.30 in the evening. The sky was now a uniform grey and there were a few snowflakes in the air. We had been on the go for over twelve hours and still had to abseil down to the col. This was out of sight, hidden by the bulging of the rock, but it certainly seemed a long way below. Once there, there was still a lot of ground to cover to the summit. The ragged skyline of serrated pinnacles seemed to be at least 200 metres above us. I turned to Jim.

'You know, I think we're getting a bit out of our depth.'

'That's what I've been thinking for the last four hours,' was his comment. That settled it. I turned to Robin.

'I'm desperately sorry, mate, but it really isn't on. We've got a good 200 metres more, quite apart from having to abseil down to the col, and I think it'd take us at least eight hours. In addition to that it looks as if the weather's breaking.'

Robin accepted my decision without a murmur. He had brought his own flag, as vice-admiral of his yacht club, and we photographed him holding it. There was just time to look around. I examined the summit mass which still towered above us. It seemed quite broken, with rock walls interspersed with talus slopes, leading up to a notched crest, where it was difficult to discern the highest point. We were at a height of 2,400 metres, as high as most of the peaks around us, and we could therefore command a superb view. Looking down the valley there was a vista of peaks, rising out of glaciers and snowfields, that stretched to the far horizon. Jim assured us that the mountains in the far distance were the Watkins Mountains, the highest in Greenland and ones that he had climbed in.

But I could barely appreciate the beauty of the scene. I was too worried about the descent and had a nagging sense of guilt. I knew how important it had been to Robin to reach the top and couldn't help feeling I had let him down. He had fulfilled his side of the bargain in getting through the ice to the coast, Jim had got us to the foot of the mountain, but I had failed to get us to the top. It brought out the difference between our situation on the boat and on the mountain. On *Suhaili* my inexperience didn't matter a jot. If I had collapsed on a bunk in the throes of seasickness, I could be a passenger and Robin would have continued to sail the boat at full efficiency and cope with any crisis that might occur. On the mountain, however, I could safeguard him with the rope, but he had to overcome each difficulty for himself, and it had been really tough on him. It was about to be tougher. Descent is always more awkward than climbing up.

So Jim soloed down first, just in front of Robin, whom I let down on the rope. On steep ground you can't see where you're putting your feet and, because you are constantly looking downwards, you become much more aware of the drop. Jim advised Robin which holds to use, while I paid out the rope that secured him. It was a slow process. Just after we had started, the sun broke through the clouds that now covered the entire sky, bathing the peaks and broken cloud to the immediate south-east in a rich, yet angry, gold. It was both beautiful and threatening, emphasising the wildness of the scene around us and our own isolation.

We abseiled down the steeper sections, but had to be immensely careful that the doubled rope could be pulled down behind us without snagging on a loose rock or pinnacle. The light was fading and it became progressively colder as we slowly picked our way down.

It was about one o'clock when we at last reached the col at the head of the wide ice slope. Jim now joined us on the rope and, with Robin in the middle, we went down one at a time, with first Jim or myself being let down on tension, walking down the ice to the end of the rope, cutting out a ledge and setting up belay points, then Robin was let down, and the last man climbed down, facing inwards, front-pointing and using his ice tools. It was a slow process and we were all so tired that we were dropping off to sleep on the stances while waiting our turn to move. It took six hours, twice the time of the ascent, to get back down to the bergschrund. At last we could unrope and stride the short distance back to the tents by six o'clock that morning. Allen and Jan had mugs of tea waiting for us. Robin produced the vodka bottle and some delicate little vodka glasses and we toasted each other.

We might not have climbed the Cathedral, but Robin's Pinnacle was almost a peak in its own right and we had had twenty-five hours of almost continuous climbing. Robin had done extraordinarily well. It wasn't his fault that the mountain had turned out to be so much more difficult than I had anticipated. Let me leave him the last word, from his tape diary recorded at his personal high point.

'From a personal point of view it's been fabulous. Some of this rock climbing's been, to say the least, a little bit worrying and I don't particularly care to be looking down vertically from about 1,200 metres, but at the same time it's exciting and I never felt actually frightened, because of the people I'm with. I've always felt very secure and I've climbed things that really I didn't think I could climb, which has been fascinating.

It's a most spectacular view from here. There are very few peaks higher than us, and looking away in the distance you just see line after line of Greenland's icy mountains. And to the south I can see the Greenland Icecap away in the distance. Nothing but white with a few lumps on it shining in the sun. It's really spectacular.

Behind me the two experts are now discussing how they're going to make the ascent next time. They've found an easier route – not less complicated but easier, if that's not a contradiction in terms. Once they've recovered from this they'll have a go for it I think. And frankly I shall do all I can to see them up there. That's what we came to do. It doesn't matter who does it. Let's hope they can manage it.'

6 Decision Time

We had been back for nearly twenty-four hours and had spent most of that time in our sleeping bags, but Jim and I had discussed our plans for another climb. We were torn between making a further attempt on the Cathedral (Point 2,660 metres) and trying the mountain that we had originally perceived to be the Cathedral (Point 2,600 metres). We had therefore decided to investigate the right-hand fork of the glacier, skiing up to the top of the headwall we had stopped short of on our first reconnaissance.

Jim stirred, raring to go.

'Come on, Chris, time to get up.'

I groaned and buried myself deeper into my sleeping bag.

'I'm too bloody tired and my neck hurts. You won't see anything anyway.' Snow had been pattering on the tent walls for some time.

Another half hour went by, and I heard the purr of the stove.

'Want a cup of tea, Chris? I think I'll go and have a look anyway. I could do with the exercise.'

I envied the energy of youth. It's the recovery time more than anything else that slows you down as you get older. At the age of twenty-six, twelve hours' rest is sufficient to bounce you back to almost full efficiency, but at the age of fifty-seven you need quite a bit more time to recover from a gruelling day, so let Jim take up the story.

> 'At about noon I started to feel restless. After all, you don't come all the way out here just to lie like a maggot in a sleeping bag reading fourteenth-century history books all day. I took a peek outside and, although the mountains around us were clad in a thin plastering of fresh snow, I was encouraged to see that the visibility had improved. So, I thought, why not go for a relaxing ski with just a light sack and some lunch and take a look at the Nameless Glacier (as we had come to refer to it) which is at the top of the right-hand fork of the glacier leading to the Cathedral. In the back of my mind, and no doubt Chris's, was the suspicion that, despite the map, the big mountain to the north was higher than the rocky Cathedral. What we needed to know was whether it was climbable from this side, in other words from the top of

the Nameless Glacier. If so, we could consider having a crack at that, instead of a second attempt at the Cathedral, though, heaven knows, we would be running seriously short of time if we changed our objective at this late stage.

What I needed was someone to come with me on my recce, and I really wanted Chris to come to give his assessment of the climbing potential. I knew he was reluctant, so I thought I'd get other volunteers first and then he'd feel left out if we all went off without him and perhaps he'd change his mind. I asked Allen first, thinking that he usually says "yes". On this occasion, though, he was feeling lazy and said "no". Jan said he'd think about it. Robin was still asleep and looked as if he needed the rest, so I tried asking Chris.

"Look," he said, "I think it's a great idea. Someone ought to go and, seeing you're so keen, I promise I'll have supper ready for you when you get back and I'll also give you some of my chocolate for being such a hero."

So I was on my own. It doesn't sound much, going off on your own, but when you do it in Greenland the sense of isolation becomes complete. All you can hear is the noise of your skis and the sound of your breath because the mountains themselves are mute. No falling rocks, no running water, just quiet.

Skiing down to the corner where the Nameless Glacier starts, I tried a few Telemark turns which look like a cross between a skier doing a snowplough and a skater doing the splits. It's a graceful and exhilarating turn when you do it properly, but with my legs and back still aching from the combined effects of load-carrying, sledge-hauling and climbing I wasn't as supple as I thought I was and fell over several times in the snowy whiteness, leaving dents in the snow at regular intervals down the glacier. I felt thankful now that Chris hadn't come because I wanted him to continue thinking I was a dab cross-country skier and not one that fell over the whole time.

At the corner, a mile or so on from the tents, I put skins on my skis and started up the Nameless Glacier. It was snowing more heavily now and beginning to drift in a veil across the narrower crevasses. Furthermore, it was gloomy and oppressive and visibility was shortening and the ski tracks I'd made were disappearing quickly. I'd better not do anything stupid, I thought, because if I plop down a crevasse now they'll never know which one.

According to the map, there should be a large mountain headwall at the top of the Nameless Glacier rather like the one we were camped underneath at the Cathedral. No such thing though. As I skied up and over the final crest of the glacier the gloomy panorama got wider and wider, until I realised that I was looking down at the Courtauld Glacier. What this meant was that I was on a col or a pass that led down into another glacier system. All very intriguing. Given more time it would have been fascinating to explore further into this new world of intricate corrie glaciers.

From the col the Cathedral was on my left and Point 2,600 metres on my right. Turning to look at the latter more closely, I quickly lost interest in climbing it, at least from this side. To do so meant descending through a complex broken ice-fall underneath the pass, across the intervening glacier, and up an equivalent icefall to the start of the climb. From there the route seemed to go up a very narrow and steep stone chute to the start of the ridge. The ridge itself looked complex with a series of rock pinnacles, or gendarmes, barring progress. Each of these would pose climbing problems of their own and the whole climb looked like it would take two or three days to complete – more days than we had to spare.

This place is always full of surprises. The land never ends up being what it seems at first sight. I sat for about fifteen minutes on my rucksack, feeling the snowflakes melt on my cheeks and gazed through the murk in the direction of the Icecap which starts in earnest about ten miles to the north. Greenland offers the explorer so much variety. There's the endless wastes of ice in the interior, all flat and featureless but with occasional solitary mountain tops called nunataks poking their heads through the ice. Casting your eyes down you can see huge valley glaciers like the Frederiksborg which we came up, or the Courtauld, the one I was now looking down at. There are all these vast ranges of mountains, too, and on the coast a whole paradise of fjords, islands, glacier fronts and icebergs. And that's without starting on the wildlife and the Greenlanders.

I started to shiver and stopped day-dreaming. The others were probably having a brew or making a radio call and I felt I'd had enough of being alone. I had achieved something however. I'd confirmed that the alluring Point 2,600 metres wasn't feasible from this side. Not this time anyway.'

Jim's information wasn't encouraging, but it meant the Cathedral itself began to seem more attractive, so we decided to go for this. We knew the route and were confident, perhaps over-confident, that we could climb it, moving quickly as a pair, without too much trouble. But I still felt desperately tired and returned to my book. I was reading *The Mammoth Hunters* by Jean Auel, the story of the lovely Ayla wandering across Siberia in the dawn of time. I had read *Clan of the Cave Bear*, the first volume of this prehistoric saga, on Everest in 1982 and had been so captivated that I read continuously by the light of a head torch through a bitterly cold −30 °C night at Advance Base Camp. It was a fascinating yet frustrating book, for the characters had a feel of suburban Americans living out some kind of Outward Bound fantasy and yet it had obviously been carefully researched. I found it compulsive escapist reading in this Greenland wilderness of rock and ice. Robin had run out of books, so I split the overweight paperback in half, while Jim perused Barbara Tuchman's magisterial history of fourteenth-century Europe.

That afternoon we had a planning session. Robin had been in daily contact with Perry on *Suhaili* and we now agreed that after spending a day filming around the bottom of the mountain, Robin, Allen and Jan would head for the coast, while Jim and I would have just one more go at the Cathedral.

I was happy to leave the complex logistics involved in rejoining *Suhaili* to Robin, while I pondered the route beyond our previous high point or escaped to the eternal triangle of tangled love connecting Ayla to Jondalar, the inarticulate all-American blond hero, and Ranee, the smooth dark ivory carver of the Mamuti.

By now I was very bored with the predictable adventures of Ayla. In any case it seemed I was a faster reader than Chris and was waiting for the next instalment, so my mind turned to the logistics of the return journey which involved two separate parties who had to be self-sufficient for an indeterminate number of days and then liaise with only one radio. We roved around the problem and eventually decided the radio should stay with me and the film crew in order to make regular contact with *Suhaili* because, whatever happened, I needed to be on board when she was moved, whether the climbers' pick-up point was to be where we had landed at the foot of the Sidegletscher or further east at Mikis Fjord. We would leave the climbers a message at the junction of Frederiksborg and Sidegletscher if they had to divert to Mikis because of ice. But if all went as we hoped and James and Perry got through Watkins Fjord in Kent's boat, we could leave the climbers the radio while we went to collect *Suhaili*. If we arrived at the Sidegletscher with *Suhaili* and found no one, we would wait. If there was no sign of Chris and Jim by 19th August we would assume they were in trouble and either come looking for them or call in an aircraft.

I wrote down the programme, including the radio frequencies, and gave it to Chris, then we swapped tents so the climbers would be undisturbed when we set out. It seemed a bit of an anti-climax when we said goodbye, as I was only moving a few metres into another tent, but for me it was a slightly emotional moment as my mind was with the climbers. We had come all this way to achieve an ascent of the Cathedral and, although I would not be with them physically, my heart and mind were there to egg them to the top.

Allen, Jan and I left just before midnight on 14th August, packing quietly so as not to wake Chris and Jim. Initially I carried a pack, while they towed pulks, since there was another pulk to collect at the base of the Cathedral valley. My progress was rather slow on the skis until I removed the skins and accepted the possibility of falling. This allowed me to keep pace with the others, we made fairly good headway and I only fell once. We were still striding along rather than gliding, but occasionally on steeper sections we let go and, for the first time on the expedition, I felt really free on the skis and began to appreciate the exhilaration that all skiers enjoy. The nights were growing noticeably darker, and we had some difficulty locating the Mitivagkat dump because snow had buried the markers. We deposited twelve days' food and two kerosene containers in an orange bag for the climbers, then redistributed our loads and were on the move again by 0300.

Two hours later we camped among the crevasses of the Frederiksborg Glacier in a force 4 wind. Although weary, I could have pressed on a little further, but the site was chosen by the others for its suitability for filming. There were mares' tails of cirrus in the sky and the wind was the strongest we had experienced for two weeks, so I shovelled snow on to the tent edge to anchor it more firmly. What happened to an insignificant little tent with three occupants if the ice shifted did not bear thinking about. However I slept soundly until Jan's alarm awoke me at 10.00 or the radio schedule with *Suhaili*. James and Perry were as cheerful as ever, James had been for another dip, voluntarily this time, to obtain close-up photographs of an iceberg. I wondered whether being almost alone on the boat in the Arctic was beginning to affect his mind. The pair of them had also showered beneath a waterfall which did nothing to reassure me concerning their sanity. The main news was that they had climbed up over the ridge on Kraemer Island to view Watkins Fjord and, although it appeared extremely jammed, they were optimistic about their chances of getting through with Kent's boat.

Allen woke me at three in the afternoon as he wanted to film me towing the pulk through the glaciers. Although the hot sun was lovely and the wind had subsided, I was not particularly keen, as the snow bridges are at their weakest in these conditions. Nevertheless, I harnessed up and began tramping round the camp and jumped the narrower crevasses. I was not encouraged by Jan's habit of filming just as I approached a crevasse and became convinced he was looking for an action shot of someone falling in. Needless to say I was careful to avoid satisfying him as there is a strict limit to the lengths I will go in the interests of art.

We breakfasted at 2200 hours and then departed. Progress was desperately slow for the first three miles as we had to zig-zag around crevasses which probably increased the distance by a factor of three and the darkness made route-finding tricky. Both Allen and I plunged through snow bridges to our waists at various times. We were not helped by the pulk harnesses which were by now very worn and kept breaking. I had started the night wearing a down jacket and windproof over a thermal vest, but quickly stripped to the vest, despite the temperature being a few degrees below zero. Once through the choss, our route was far from easy as the glacial rivers, which had caused problems on the way up to the Cathedral, were now on average half a metre deeper, and our detours brought us to two small lakes. By this time we were beyond caring about such obstacles and just waded straight through with the pulks floating behind. Then we were climbing up the approach to the Sidegletscher.

Jan and Allen wanted to camp, but I had my second wind and was keen to ensure I could give Perry a definite time to meet us. So we continued upwards to the highest part of the glacier. We had covered eight and a half miles as the crow flies, but must have travelled over twice that distance. Since our route was now all downhill from this camp, I confidently told Perry to rendezvous at the foot of the glacier at 0900 hours the next morning. In the evening I called Portishead and raised them on the aircraft commercial frequencies, but although they came through loud and clear, my signal was too weak for a satisfactory conversation.

We started late that night, not until 0215 on the morning of the 17th. We had planned an earlier departure but I was learning that climbers and their associates are not very speedy at getting underway. However it was not important, as we quickly skied down to the crevasses at the turn of the glacier where, because of an ineffective snowplough, I had to fall over in order to stop promptly when Jan shouted that I was about to pile into a crevasse.

After a two-week absence it was quite amazing to see how the terrain had altered. The moraine which ran alongside the glacier at the camp site had disappeared and the crevasses were significantly larger, some up to three metres wide. Luckily rain had washed away the surface snow, so they were easy to spot. We parked the sledges in a position where Jim and Chris would see them and, loading everything we could carry into our packs, set off towards the fjord's edge. Walking over the scrambled rock was as unpleasant as I remembered, but when we were over half a mile from the landing point we heard a distant call and there was the red boat creeping in towards us, right on time.

It was great to see Perry and James again. The gear went into the boat but, before leaving, we dumped a prominent bag of assorted goodies plus the radio for Chris and Jim. I hoped to return with *Suhaili* in time to greet them but, in case of hold ups, they would at least have a few creature comforts.

On the way back to *Suhaili,* manoeuvring competently through the ice, Perry and James told us how their survey was almost complete. On several days they had accompanied Kent on his forays and learned a good deal about the area and its possible but rather alarming development plans. A gold-bearing stratum, which extends from Skrgrd to Mikis, contains five parts in a million of gold, almost enough for profitable exploitation. This would bring a small town of 3,000 people into the region and involve crushing 20,000 tons of rock a day. Kent was not at all sure he had done the right thing by drawing the world's attention to the gold and, although Greenland urgently needs trade, we could not help feeling depressed by the potential destruction such an industry would cause in this unspoilt wilderness. The current world price of gold ensures the project is uneconomical at present, but now the prospectors are also searching for platinum.

We were into Suhaili Bugt by 1400 hours and there she was, safe and sound, but lying a little to the east of where I left her. Perry explained that the previous position was very uncomfortable and they had moved but decided, very sensibly, not to inform me as they knew I would fuss. Apart from this, the only alarms had come in the form of wandering bergs which had drifted in, despite the narrowness of the entrance. The solution to this problem had been to put the nose of the rubber dinghy against any threatening bergs and drive them out of the bay. Of the dreaded katabatic pitarac wind there was no sign and the strongest wind was about force 4. Interestingly, they had had very little fog, whereas two miles away Kent was frequently fogbound.

After unpacking the equipment, I treated myself to a luxurious hot wash, donned fresh clothing and was very happy to be back on board. We were interrupted when two sleek kayaks swept into the bay expertly paddled by two small hunters. They pulled alongside and I saw a rifle and harpoon stowed handily on deck. One, who had spent six years in Denmark, spoke excellent English and we discovered these were the people who intended wintering in the camp nearby. They were off to hunt seals and narwhals and offered a narwhal tusk of pure ivory, over two metres long, for £400. All of us were against whale hunting in any form, but it is difficult to take a strong moral stand with a threatened people who know no other living but the one they have followed for centuries.

We debated whether to use Kent's boat for collecting the climbers but decided against. It was not sufficiently spacious to transport all the gear and nobody fancied living on it if Chris and Jim were late. Also it lacked a powerful radio which might be essential in an emergency. So our main task for the remainder of the day was fitting the large baulks of timber around the bow in preparation for the passage to the Sidegletscher. The solution to holding the wood in place was to lash one end of each piece to the bobstay and then run a bridle under the hull to keep the after ends at the waterline, while additional lines were led from the after ends to the deck. Satisfied at last, we checked the moorings and then enjoyed a Happy Hour. As the sun disappeared behind the nearby mountains, the temperature dropped below zero immediately and I appreciated Perry and James's comments about having the cabin heater at full blast and the hatch battened down. We ate proper food at last for our evening meal in the cosiness of the cabin and turned in early.

On the 18th we were up at 0300 and sorted out the moorings while a greasy breakfast was prepared – fried eggs after a fortnight without were a delight. At 0500 we motored into Kangerdlugssuaq Fjord and a northerly force 4. This was our first taste of a real wind in the fjords and we were keen to observe the reaction of the ice. It was moving southwards, and certainly would have piled up against any piece of land in its way, but the actual movement through the water was very slight. Fortunately, the wind died away to nearly nothing within two hours and the sails we had set were stowed. The ice was even worse than the previous day and long before the junction with Watkins Fjord we were crawling along and cautiously picking our way through a huge mass of small bergy bits interspersed with large bergs. The timbers on the bows helped a little but, as we had feared, most of the ice extended below the surface and so hit the hull before the fenders. This did not augur well for Watkins Fjord and, when it eventually came into view after four hours, it looked a nightmare. If it were not for Chris and Jim, I would never have ventured inside with *Suhaili*, as apart from the ice situation, the wind might spring up from any direction at any time and the tide was ebbing fast and driving us back down the fjord.

It was ten hours before we covered the four miles to the camp. Ten hours of intense concentration by everyone, conning, steering and fending off ice. We were constantly stopping, waiting for bergs to part so we could squeeze through and, although each pause provided the excuse for a brew up, we fretted at the delay and I think we all worried as to whether we would ever get out. Once again we edged slowly across to the north side to be free of the large bergs and adverse current – the ebb seemed to be endless – and finally spotted the moraine when it was nearly two miles away. Our advance was slightly faster on this side, mainly because we could afford to barge the smaller pieces of ice, but still poor in comparison with the previous approach. Shortly after 1700 hours the radio crackled into life and Chris's voice came over, just recognisable as the range was too close for the frequency. But what really mattered was that they were safe and had arrived at the camp. We told them we were only a mile away and shortly before 1900 anchored as far inshore as we dared. I had not chosen the camp site well as only 200 metres away the glacier entered the fjord and might choose to calve more bergs at any moment and create God knows what sort of wave. But at least the team was reunited and we could hear about Chris and Jim's adventures.

7 The Second Attempt

Our tent, some 450 metres below, was little more than a dot on the surface of the snow basin, and empty now, for Robin, Allen and Jan had left for the coast the previous night while Jim and I were still asleep. We had set out at four o'clock that morning and all my doubts and fatigue had dropped away in the exhilaration of free upward movement. We were climbing unroped, each going at his own pace, taking his own path, crampons biting into the ice, the axes acting as little more than a point of balance. From the col we continued unroped, enjoying the occasional awkward step, like little boulder problems on the way. It was only seven o'clock when we reached the shoulder, seven hours faster than on our first attempt. We had already decided to bypass the pinnacle by abseiling into the gully which was now in deep shade. You could only glimpse its snow-covered bed, the headwall being concealed by the jutting rocks of the pinnacle, but I had it in my mind that it would be snow all the way to the col.

We had a quick drink of water and munched a chocolate bar before placing a big loop, chopped from the spare rope I had given the others for their return to the coast, round a large block on the crest of the ridge. Through it I threaded our abseil rope and started down. Fresh snow covered steel hard ice on which my crampons barely made an impression. There is something very committing about abseiling down a section on an ascent. It raises the question of how you are going to get back up it on your return and brings memories of the *Hinterstoisser Traverse* on the North Wall of the Eiger, when all the climbers perished because they had failed to leave a back rope and couldn't reverse their route. We didn't have a spare rope to leave.

The scale of everything was bigger than it looked. The doubled fifty-metre ropes just reached a shelf of piled snow that snaked round the corner, still well above the bed of the couloir. I was already traversing out at an angle, the rope threatening to swing me back in a gigantic pendulum as I kicked into the hard ice. I hacked a foothold, inserted an ice screw and called Jim to join me. Once there, we pulled the rope down behind us. We were committed and would have to climb back up that steep hard ice at the end of a long day when we were already tired.

Jim led on down to the end of the shelf, clambering over snow-plastered granite blocks. We were now poised some twenty-two metres above the bed of the gully. I abseiled again, worried by the steepness of the line. It was actually overhanging and every crack was jammed with ice. Could we climb back on the return? In the base of the couloir the ice, covered by a few inches of insubstantial fresh snow, was as hard as ever. It was like an alpine north face in the depths of winter. The sun never touched the retaining walls, and only reached the bed of the deep fissure for a short time each day. It dropped away steeply below me and I could see the basin from where we had started that morning, some 620 metres below, framed between the sheer walls.

Glancing up, I saw that the chasm reared up into a rocky headwall, above which flowed a great bulge of overhanging yellow-green ice. Jim abseiled to join me and I pulled the rope through once again. We were now fully committed. I could at least see an ice-filled groove just off vertical that seemed to give us an avenue of escape on our return.

I started up the ice to the beginning of the headwall which was broken by a series of basalt dykes. It towered skywards, threatening and daunting. There were no cracks wide enough for nut protection and when I tried to hammer a piton into a hairline crack, it bottomed almost immediately. The rock was either smooth compact basalt or shattered granite. I moved hesitantly, uncomfortably aware of our isolation. Trapped in this dark cleft we were totally alone. The others by this time would be at least fifteen miles down the glacier and we were without any means of communication except our emergency radio beacon back in the tent at the foot of the Cathedral.

I was heading for some piled blocks which provided a reasonable stance, hammered in an angle piton, and brought Jim up to join me.

'Do you want a go out in front?' I asked.

'It's all right, you might as well stay in the lead. You'll be quicker,' was the reply.

I didn't mind. I love leading and the next pitch was both alluring and daunting and looked even steeper than it had from below. I started up an icy groove with the basalt rib on one side and smooth featureless granite on the other. I was soon fifteen metres above Jim. There were no cracks. I tried to hammer a piton into a hairline but it bounced out and fell, tinkling away down the gully. I eased myself upwards. The rib offered no positive holds, just rounded, sloping shelves which gave no grip for my hands and on which my crampon points skidded. I carefully tapped a peg into a horizontal break, but the tone of the blows was flat and dull, sure signs of a poor placement. I was now about twenty metres above Jim, had no good runners and was just below the final surge of rock before the col. I had my shoulder against the great teardrop of ice and was ineffectively trying to find a placement for a good running belay, while trying to work out a sequence of moves to take me above the bulge. But there was no security, no handholds and the prospect of a long, probably fatal, fall if I came off. Time goes very quickly in these circumstances, and I realised I had been in the same place for about half an hour. I hadn't admitted it to myself but I was stuck.

For the second time goes all too slowly. Jim had plenty of time to contemplate the consequences of a fall and was getting steadily colder as he stamped up and down on top of the blocks that formed a precarious stance. Eventually he called out.

'Why not try the wall behind you? You might be able to use the ice.'

I was focused on to the basalt rib in front of me, but now shifted my balance, edged round and suddenly with a new perspective, realised I could insert an ice screw. I rescued my ice hammer from its holster and took a swing at the ice with the pick. It went in with a reassuring crunch, I could at last hang on to something and scrabbled with my free hand at my waist harness for a screw. I had trouble unclipping it from the karabiner.

'Damn the thing. Come on, Bonington, calm down,' I told myself. I took a few breaths, managed to get it undipped and then tried to screw it into the ice. These screws have stainless steel tips, are designed to be hand-placed and screwed, but you still have to get a placement in the smooth ice. My hand was shaking with fatigue but I persisted and at last I could feel a resistance as the screw engaged, carving out its own thread. After several rests the head of the screw was at last flush with the ice. I clipped in a karabiner, dragged up the rope, clipped that in, and suddenly felt very different. I was secure, relaxed in my bridged position and it all began to seem feasible. I managed to get a purchase with my ice hammer in my right hand, a flat shelving rock hold for my left, kicked into the overhanging ice with the front points of the crampons on my right foot and bridged out with my left on to the smooth, slippery rock. Another two moves and I was poised precariously on the brink of the col. Through my widely bridged legs I could see the little white blob of Jim's face far below. Another heave, left hand plunged into fresh soft snow, and I was on the col. I let out a whoop of joy. I'd made it and the climbing had been everything you could want. Scottish Grade V, precarious, frightening, and I'd come through it. I dumped my sack, found a belay and hauled in the rope.

I had plenty of time to assess our situation while Jim followed up the pitch. It was now midday. We had taken nearly five hours to bypass the pinnacle, but we were still hardly any higher than we had been at the shoulder from which we had abseiled all that time before. Even so, looking up at the back wall of the pinnacle, I congratulated myself on having taken the right decision. It was overhanging for much of the way, with every crack jammed with ice and every ledge covered in snow. Abseiling down it we should have been lucky to have landed on the tiny, almost knife-edge col, and getting back up would have been even more desperate.

Jim arrived panting. 'Good lead that. Glad I let you do it.'

A rocky groove stretched above. It was just off vertical but seemed to have plenty of holds.

'Might as well take the rope off and climb this solo,' I suggested.

Once we'd coiled the ropes, Jim set out first and I followed him closely. It was good to move swiftly and easily on rock once again. The groove led up to a boulder field and then on to a more broken but steepening crag. We decided to put the rope on, and I led another rocky scoop that proved easier than it looked. We'd climbed a good 100 metres, but were still not level with the top of Robin's Pinnacle. It was indeed a peak in its own right.

We were now confronted by a further boulder field and rock step, this time steeper still. Surely we must be getting somewhere near the top. The deep gash in front of us leaked icicles. I had no desire to try that and therefore traversed below the wall on to the top of a big boulder and pulled up on to a rib to find myself on the edge of a deep-cut gully. I didn't like the look of that either, so followed a sloping shelf back to the right which led to the foot of yet another overhanging chimney. But the wall looked feasible. It was steep but there were some holds leading to a flake suspended like the legendary *Sword of Damocles*. Time to bring Jim up.

Once he'd belayed, I started up the wall. The rock was a flaky granite and even though there were cracks for nut runners behind blocks, I was afraid a fall would simply pull the block out to land it and me on top of Jim. I climbed hesitantly, first trending fearfully right towards the dank depths of the chimney, and then venturing straight up but abandoned that course when it became necessary to heave on the *Sword of Damocles*. I then looked out to the left. A line of foot-holds and a flat rounded ledge reached out to a nose of rock where the angle eased. I needed some good protection and hammered a peg into a crack. It gave a reassuring ringing tone. Even so, I hammered it into its head, and then hammered it some more. It was time to commit myself. I placed a foot tentatively on the rounded crumbling granite of the ledge and reached my hands across on to a higher sloping ledge. As I shifted my weight across my foot slipped and one hand-hold crumbled away, but somehow I managed to stay in contact with the rock, balanced across, stepped up and I was on a sloping ledge. A wide crack and inclined gangway led back to the right and the top of the wall. I was slow, not because it was difficult, but because I was frightened.

It was all reminiscent of Derbyshire gritstone, technically about a Stanage VS, but in big double boots with a rucksack I was increasingly aware of our isolation and my own fatigue. Jim followed quickly to the peg, spent ten minutes hammering at it before abandoning it at my urging, and we scrambled through the boulders to gaze on yet another rock step. This must be the last wall, surely. We peered round the corner to the left, but it all looked steep and bulging. The prow in front of us had a groove with a crack that at least gave promise of holds and protection. I opted for that and started up it. After about twelve metres it reared steeply out of sight to the right. I had run out of courage and needed the reassurance that there was a continuation of the line round the corner. So

I asked Jim if he could unrope and scramble up a little pinnacle on the end of the rock shoulder on which he was belayed to have a look. He climbed out to the edge.

'Do you want the good news or the bad news first?' he asked.

'Let's have the good.'

'Well, there is a line to the top of the pinnacle you're on,' he shouted, 'but I'm afraid it's not the highest one. There seem to be about five more that are higher.'

At that stage all I could absorb was the fact there was a way up round the corner and I started out once again. A hand-jamming crack led into the shade, where every flat or sloping surface was covered in powder snow. I was climbing a pile of steep, precariously balanced blocks, my numb hands tunnelling into the snow, and was now a long way above my last runner. A final heave brought me on to a comfortable sized ledge. Jim climbed up to join me and I suggested he led on up to the top. In spite of what Jim had told me, I still somehow thought of the summit being the top of this pinnacle, and it wasn't until I reached it that I registered there was indeed another higher tower just beyond, and then another and another and another.

'We'll have to make this our summit,' Jim announced. 'It's six o'clock, we've been going for fourteen hours and I think it could take another eight to get across these.'

He was so sure of his decision. I felt numb with a sense of anti-climax combined with tiredness. I muttered, prevaricated and studied the serrated gendarmes. They looked steep and forbidding. Part of me wanted to go on and probably would have done had Jim had a blind enthusiasm. But he was right. We had no bivvy gear, were already low on water, were tired and very aware of our isolation.

'If you really want to go on, I'll go with you,' Jim said.

I looked at the far pinnacle. It was about 200 metres away and maybe twenty or thirty metres higher than where we stood, but there were five more towers in between. The sky was now overcast and the cold was beginning to bite. I didn't really want to go on.

'No, you're right. Let's go down.'

But first we had something to eat, finished our water and gazed around us. To the south-west we could see the Courtauld Glacier flowing down to the Courtauld Fjord and Kangerdlugssuaq. The mountains to the south, reaching towards Mejslen, were a jumble of ice and rock peaks offering the climber endless variety and challenge, while to the north, tantalising, was the stately pyramid of Point 2,600 metres, that certainly looked every bit as high as us, if not higher.

Our sense of frustration and unfulfillment was overlaid with the very real worry of making a safe descent. It was time to go. We scrambled down to the edge of the nose and I started to hunt for a good anchor point from which to make our first abseil. It was around ten o'clock that night when we reached the bed of the gully. This was the part that I dreaded. In the gloom of the twilight, exaggerated by the dark confines of the cleft, the ice runnel I had picked out as a possible escape seemed both steeper and thinner. I borrowed Jim's ice hammer to give myself two tools, put on my crampons and started up it. It was just off vertical. The ice was hard and brittle, breaking off in big dinner plates and the rock on either side of the groove bulged out, pushing me off balance. I managed to get a piton into a crack, which gave me some reassurance, and edged my way up, placed a sling over a small spike of rock to the side, straddled out and ended up standing on the spike of rock. Even though it was bitterly cold, I was now sweating profusely, panting with effort and fear.

'You might like to have a go at this,' I yelled down to Jim. 'I'm shattered, I'm not sure I can make it.'

'You can do it, Chris, just keep at it.'

I did. My call of despair was more rhetorical than anything else.

I hammered away at the ice, getting secure placements for my tools, kicked into the steep ice, bridged out on to the rock at the side and at last heaved up on to the ledge. It was even harder for Jim to follow, since I had battered most of the ice at the back of the groove. He climbed on through over the broken snow-covered ledges that gave on to the steep ice slope which provided the final barrier. I was hoping he would lead it. I'd run out of strength and nerve. But Jim stopped at its foot, took a belay and brought me up. Nothing was said, but he obviously expected me to lead it.

I was very, very slow. It was straight forward enough – 60 °C ice covered by a six-centimetre layer of soft snow – but the ice was hard and brittle and I was desperately tired. I put in one of my ice screws every seven metres or so. I barely had the strength to do it, but felt the need of their security.

At last I reached the top and brought Jim up. We were out of the trap, back on familiar, comparatively easy ground, but it was one o'clock in the morning and in the dark twilight that prevailed we could barely distinguish the holds on the rock.

'It'd be worth stopping for an hour or so until it's a bit lighter,' suggested Jim.

I concurred. The thought of a rest was welcome. We scrambled down to some sloping scree-covered ledges, uncoiled the ropes to act as insulation from the cold rocks beneath, took our boots off, put our feet in our rucksacks and tried to sleep. My clothing and socks were soaked in sweat but we were already wearing everything we had. I was so tired I could barely eat the little food we had left. Curled into a foetal position, I tried to conserve what warmth was left in my body.

Jim, who had to suffer my snores, told me I slept for about an hour, but on waking I was shivering uncontrollably. Jim decided I was in the first throes of hypothermia, and I was just aware of the urgency of his voice telling me to get up and pack my sack. As I started moving ponderously down behind him, some warmth began to come back into my body. The anchor points from our previous descent were already in place and we now made good progress to the col at the top of the ice slope by 5.00 a.m.

There just remained ten rope-lengths to the bottom. I'd had enough of leading. I never like reversing ice at the best of times, and so I asked Jim to let me down on the rope so that he could follow. I let him lower me, walking and stumbling straight down the ice to the end of the rope, hacking out holds, putting in ice screws and taking in the rope as Jim came down, facing inwards, but moving so quickly that it was all I could do to keep up with the rope as I paid it though my figure of eight descendeur. The angle eased towards the bottom, and I felt sufficiently confident to climb down unroped. Half an hour later we were both at the foot of the slope and a run down hard easy-angled snow took us to the tent we had left twenty-eight hours earlier.

I was too tired to do more than drink the brew of tea that Jim prepared and then dropped into a deep sleep. We woke in the early evening, cooked a huge meal and talked through the previous day's climb. I no longer had that sense of disappointment I had experienced at our high point. It had been a superb climb. My exhaustion and near hypothermia were good enough justification for our retreat. I had only just made it out of the deep-cut gully on the way back, but the climb had been a good one and Jim had been a great partner. We'd pushed ourselves to the limit and had taken a sensible decision in the circumstances.

My principal mistake had been in underestimating the time the climb would take. Had we carried lightweight bivouac equipment (which we had not in fact brought on the expedition) we could have rested for an hour or so at our high point, had a warm drink and then completed the climb. But Jim had never had to bivouac on any of his many Greenland climbs before, though he had always been climbing a month or so earlier, when there was a genuine twenty-four hours of daylight. He also commented that this was by far the most difficult climb he had tackled in Greenland.

We still had plenty to do. It was now 16th August and we were due to reach Watkins Fjord on the 18th, the date we had hoped Robin would be able to pick us up in *Suhaili*. It was essential he did so that day in order to fulfil his side of the bargain with Kent Brooks to tow Kent's aluminium boat and team of scientists round to Mikis Fjord for their flight out from Greenland. I reflected how different the tight schedules of modern adventurers were from the timescale on which Lawrence Wager operated in 1935-6 when he had come to the Watkins Mountains and had explored the Frederiksborg Glacier with provisions, not just for the year he planned to be away, but for a second year, if it proved necessary. He had also brought his wife along. Perhaps he would not have been so relaxed about the passing months if he had left her behind.

We set out at dawn on 17th August. I felt surprisingly rested. The snow was in good condition and we were able to glide most of the way down the glacier to its junction with the Frederiksborg, where the others had left a food dump. We picked this up and continued down the glacier, weaving our way round the open crevasses. It became rougher and the snow thinner, until we were forced to take off skis and start walking, jumping the surface streams and heaving the pulks over the broken ridges of ice. I was surprised how fit I felt and was absurdly flattered when Jim told me I was the only person he had ever skied with who could keep up with him.

The next twenty-four hours grew progressively soggier as the rain set in. We camped in the hope it would stop. It didn't and we were soaked before we reached the broad col leading down to the Sidegletscher and the gear dump. Stomping down the moraine skirting the glacier snout, we saw a little red blob on the top of a boulder down by the fjord. It was one of our duffel bags filled with cans of beer, freshly baked bread, cheese, fresh apples and even oranges. We pitched our sodden tent, climbed into damp sleeping bags and savoured our feast. It needed real effort to get back into wet clothes, go out, set up the aerial and tune the radio to call Robin who was picking his way towards us through dense ice in Watkins Fjord. We had already begun to ferry the gear dump down to the shore as we saw *Suhaili* nosing her way round the point and chugging slowly into the little bay below the glacier snout. Robin, displaying his characteristic reliability and seamanship, had reached us right on time.

We piled everything on board, tying the pulks to the roof of the cabin, and leaving gear and clothing in sodden heaps. I crawled into the slot against the port bulkhead, cocooned in my damp sleeping bag, and fell asleep almost immediately to the throb of the engine and calls from on deck, as Robin conned *Suhaili* back through the ice. I no longer had any responsibility. He was in charge and had my absolute trust. I could just sleep and sleep and sleep.

8 The Return

Though I had feared it, no bergs calved from Sidegletscher while I waited for the others to arrive back with the last of the equipment. But large chunks, floating along the glacier's clifflike edge, drifted up to *Suhaili* and it was she who moved when I shoved at them with an oar. Apart from this, it was really rather pleasant to be alone for a short while, admire the scenery, which retained its magical fascination, and dream of maybe returning some day. However the ice was rapidly piling up across the fjord's entrance and since this was our only escape route, I watched the movement with growing apprehension. As I could not see far enough to obtain a proper impression from the spreaders, I took the dinghy to inspect the beach and assess the depth of water. If the ice did close in, the last resort lay in manoeuvring *Suhaili* inshore until she almost grounded and hope this way to avoid being crushed.

I beached the dinghy and scrambled to the top of the moraine for a better view. From here I could see that beyond the nearby bergs the ice was moving down the fjord with the tide in ever greater quantities, and already the track we came in by was totally blocked. As I stowed some gear into the dinghy, I considered whether I should shift *Suhaili's* anchorage, but taking her through the ice alone would be tricky and result in a longer portage for the shore party, so I decided to stay put and, to take my mind off the problem, I went back for another consignment from the camp. I was just completing a third trip when the others appeared, having completed an arduous portage in under two hours.

We loaded at high speed, if throwing everything on to the deck can be called loading, and were underway at 2100 hours after freeing the anchor from beneath a berg which had drifted right over it. Initially we were forced to motor eastwards and deeper into the fjord to bypass the ice jam around the moraine, weaving frantically and forcing a passage in places. I winced as we crunched through the gaps where the ice extended below the water and beneath our timber defences. But by this stage I was prepared to take risks to escape. Perhaps it was tiredness, we had been on the go for sixteen hours, or the light mist and low cloud which had been absent for over two weeks, but the ice seemed thoroughly menacing now, a feeling I had not experienced during our earlier incursions. If the wind rose it could have a disastrous effect. Tilman lost a boat due to ice and wind driving him ashore 300 miles to the south when close to habitation and assistance, and anyone who has seen the film of Shackleton's *Endurance* being crushed by ice in the Antarctic in 1915 will sympathise with my desperation to reach clearer water.

Perry, James and I took turns steering, conning from the mast and fending in a routine that on our fourth traverse through the fjord was well honed. Although there was a dusk, there was sufficient light to pick a way through the thick ice patches throughout the night. Once we had rounded the moraine, we headed obliquely to the fjord's centre where the ebbing current, running at more than half a knot, assisted our passage and to my immense relief we finally emerged from Watkins Fjord shortly after midnight. Unfortunately, the heavy ice had drifted well into Kangerdlugssuaq Fjord and initially progress there was not exactly speedy, but gradually, as a reward for our continuing efforts, conditions improved and we crept into Suhaili Bugt just after 0400 hours. We anchored with a running moor, first dropping one anchor and releasing its entire scope of chain, and then another and hauling back on the first so we were equidistant. This held *Suhaili* nicely and prevented her swinging around. Confident of the boat's safety, we crashed on to the cabin floor as all four usable bunks were occupied, but it could have been a bed of nails for all we cared.

Movement close by woke me shortly after 1000 hours and we made a thoroughly unhealthy breakfast of skirlie, fried corned beef with eggs, and over coffee worked out a programme. Top priority was to try in vain once more to contact Portishead. Then we needed to return Kent's many favours to us by collecting two geologists camped on Kraemer Island and transporting them to Kent's camp where we had promised to take his boat in tow for the twenty-mile run to Mikis Fjord. So we said farewell to Suhaili Bugt which had served us so well.

Kent's camp was only a short distance away in Hjemsted Bugt and to reach it we had to pass the Inuit settlement. Their corrugated iron shacks were so badly erected that it seemed a puff of wind might flatten them, let alone a heavy fall of snow. The impression was not improved by the profusion of ancient oil drums littering the surrounding area. Presumably it was not worth the effort and cost of returning the empties to Angmagssalik, so they lay around until they rusted away. We were informed that there were four families in residence, but the washing lines and numbers of children indicated this was inaccurate, or the Inuit population is nothing like as threatened as rumoured.

However, if the houses were ramshackle, the opposite was true of the boats. These consisted of fast, well maintained fibreglass power boats on moorings, and smaller dinghies and kayaks ashore. Everyone came out to wave and shout as we went by as, although some of the men had paddled round to visit us, this was the first opportunity for most to see a yacht so far north. Perry piloted me between two small islands inhabited by packs of huskies and into the fjord where Kent was packed and loaded. As soon as we had attached a tow line to the red boat, he joined us on board and we declared the first Happy Hour for the complete team for nearly three weeks.

The wind was light from the west so there was no point in sailing and we motored past towering sea cliffs which Chris examined with a professional eye, but I could only view as a potentially dangerous lee shore. There were giant icebergs lying across the entrance to Kangerdlugssuaq Fjord but the number out at sea had declined since we had first arrived, so our passage was straightforward and Mikis Fjord opened up shortly after 2000 hours. In contrast to Kangerdlugssuaq it was narrow, running between steep high mountains and, to our delight, relatively ice-free. Low cloud on the mountain tops gave the place a gloomy appearance, the silence was oppressive and, half-closing one's eyes, one could imagine a Viking longboat rowing along with a Kirk Douglas-type in the prow blowing a long ox horn. After two miles the fjord widened and turned sharply to the right where the slopes were gentler and covered with scree to at least 500 metres. There were scattered icebergs within this area but, compared to Kangerdlugssuaq, it was virtually empty and explains why the fjord is under consideration as the port for the gold extraction works. It was here in 1930 that Watkins' party brought the *Quest* to offload the Moth float plane to undertake aerial photography.

Our objective was the Sodalen Glacier where we were to drop off the geologists for an aircraft pick-up. On the way we grounded twice on shallows where the moraine extended under water but refloated without difficulty as the bottom was soft mud. While anchoring, the radio, which was tuned to the BBC World Service, told us of President Gorbachev's overthrow and the international reaction. This provoked an energetic discussion with Chris and me explaining to the younger members that, whereas no one was likely to require the services of fifty-plus-year-old tank commanders and mines weeping officers, we had a duty to rush them home to be called up! Once anchored, with fourteen metres beneath *Suhaili's* keel, Kent ferried his boat into the lagoon and he and his colleagues began offloading their gear. Then we helped carry the red boat well above high water mark and turn it over to await his return. Like so many who love Greenland, he had no intention of allowing his new post at Muscat University to prevent him coming back. In fact, he was already making plans. The shore party, which now included Allen Jewhurst as we had no room for him aboard, had three hours to scale the glacier for their rendezvous with the aircraft, so we said goodbye and, once back on *Suhaili,* weighed anchor and headed down the fjord.

I had not received a decent weather forecast for a while, so we tidied the boat and prepared properly for sea as we went along. There were wisps of cirrus, indicating strong winds at high levels, so we prepared for rough weather, just in case. Once out of Mikis Fjord our path looked fairly berg-free, although there were many growlers about and a good look out was essential. To allow everyone plenty of rest, I connected up the Autohelm and set watches of one and a half hours on, seven and a half off. We reverted easily to the routine, the mountaineers remembering their sailing lessons and able now to take their watches alone. The weather was kind, the wind never exceeded force 1, and dinner was an all hands affair. We were still washing up when the sun set just after 2200 hours. It did not reappear again until 0600 on the 21st, which demonstrated how the nights had lengthened during our visit.

The wind was now just west of south, which put us on a close-hauled course for Reykjavik in the south-east corner of Iceland, but the choppy sea quickly made this impossible, as we were forced off the wind and I started to examine alternative ports. As the glass was falling, it seemed a depression was sweeping into the Denmark Strait and it was therefore prudent to dive for cover. I plot-ted a course just north of Snæfellsjökull at the southern end of Breidhafjördhur, a large bay north of Reykjavik. By 2000 hours our position showed we were not going to make our objective, the wind was force 7 which created too much leeway, so we headed for Patreksfjördhur, further to the north. At 0100 on 22nd August, and down to the jib and mizzen, this destination was also slip-ping away to windward, so I chose the next fjord north, Arnarfjördhur, which is nearly the north-westernmost point of Iceland. If the wind continued to strengthen I was considering abandoning all attempts to reach Reykjavik, sail around the north of Iceland and somehow drop Jan at a port on the way. In ret-rospect, this would have been a wise choice and we would probably have arrived home a lot sooner.

In common with all approaches described by the *Admiralty Pilot*, a gloomy picture was painted of indifferent anchorages and off-shore winds in Arnarfjördhur and very violent squalls attacked us as we passed the entrance. I was alone at the helm and had to hang on tightly as we heeled over more than 60°.

The *Admiralty Pilot* is badly in need of updating for much of the Icelandic coast, and Bildudalur has grown considerably from being the mere trading post it is described as. There were a number of small boats in the harbour, secured behind reassuringly solid sea walls, and we made fast to one of them. Although we flew the Q flag, no one was interested. There was probably no official for miles, so we went ashore for a hefty Scandinavian breakfast and telephone calls, and Jan found himself a local air service to fly him to Reykjavik to rejoin Allen.

The rest of us slept late the next morning, in part due to an excellent dinner in a café which did not object to us bringing our own wine. Then we topped up the fuel tanks and, after an expensive last shop for fresh provisions, decided to take advantage of lighter winds to head south. We should have realised from the presence of a small Russian fishing boat at anchor off the port that further bad weather was on its way, but we were keen to press on. We were, however, about to learn why Iceland was originally colonised – it is an easy place to sail to, but can be all but impossible to leave. The wind was still funnelling into the fjord and it took us five hours to make the open sea. Once free of Arnarfjördhur, the wind was a light south westerly and we were able to speed at up to five and a half knots. But that evening the forecast reported a storm moving our way at eight knots, so I thought it prudent to run for cover before we felt its effects. The morning sky was ominously pink and, with a backing and rising wind, told us the next depression was almost upon us, so we altered course toward the splendid extinct volcano of Snæfellsjökull, invisible in the low cloud. The only sheltered haven in the vicinity seemed to be at Rifsovn, inside Breidhafjördhur, and we were relieved to find it was almost totally enclosed by the land and a substantial sea wall.

We spent the next three days in Rifsovn. All the fishing boats had been ordered into port and even within the harbour, where the fetch was little more than 150 metres, the waves were whipped up and spindrift was flying everywhere. Our lines had to be constantly checked for wear as we heeled to the gusts, sometimes sufficiently strong to drive the gunwale underwater, although we were in the lee of the quay and a fishing boat. An enormous bang on the 27th sent us rushing on deck to discover that a particularly violent gust had snapped off all the wind generator's blades, scoring the deck with indentations of over a centimetre and one had shot straight into the radar reflector. We made plans to climb Snæfellsjökull and I was keen to discover exactly where near here Eric the Red had sailed from on his voyage to Greenland a thousand years ago but we ended up eating very expensive fish and chips and running a mean canasta school. I expected the climbers to chafe at the delay. But Chris was notably philosophical.

'I quite enjoyed our stay at Rifsovn. Waiting for an improvement in the weather was something I was accustomed to. Admittedly, I was now anxious to get home and occasionally thought how easy it would be to get a flight from the neighbouring air strip to Reykjavik and be in Glasgow that same afternoon. But I was never really tempted. It had become very important to finish the voyage with this little group with whom I had been in closer proximity than I would have been on a mountaineering expedition. There were books to read, games to play, a walk over the windswept turf or expensive cups of coffee in the little café by the harbour. There was no point in fretting; we had to wait for the wind.'

On 28th August the wind veered westerly and reduced to force 5. The larger fishing boats set off for sea at mid-morning and, as the next predicted depression was about 700 miles away, we decided to follow suit and sailed in the afternoon. I allowed 15° for leeway on account of the heavy swell, but with the jib, three reefed main, and mizzen, we were soon making between five and six knots. We rounded Cape Reykjanes at 0720 on the 29th and set course for the north of Scotland, but within two hours the wind died and then swung round from the east. By 1600 it was force 5 and rising and it was obvious we lacked sufficient sea-room to ride out the gale if we continued, so we reluctantly retreated once more, this time towards Reykjanes. I did consider trying one of the new fishing ports on the southern coast but the details are sparse in the *Pilot* and we were without a large-scale chart. By 2000 hours we were under jib only and running before a full gale, the waves were mounting in size and breaking, which gave the crew experience in handling a heavy boat in big seas – and they learned what I have discovered over the last twenty-eight years, that *Suhaili* is a wonderful little sea boat.

> 'I had been crouching at the side of the cockpit for two hours when we headed back for Reykjanes. I was sharing the watch with Robin and for a time had taken the helm. It had been strangely exciting, butting through the seas with the breaking white-topped waves chasing down behind us. All the sails were now reefed and we had even dropped the boom so that it rested on the roof of the cabin to offer as little wind resistance as possible, as we clawed our way along the southern coast towards the projecting spur of Reykjanes, which jutted out into the sea like one side of a trap for the unwary sailor. It was difficult to hold the course and the compass card swirled from side to side as the waves smashed into *Suhaili* from the beam. I couldn't help feeling a sense of relief when Robin took over the helm. Then all I could do was keep him company, feeling trickles of water penetrate the outer defences of my jacket and seep down my neck, as the bow smashed into the troughs, and the cabin gave a little protection from the solid sheets of spray that swept the decks.
>
> The clouds hung low and every few minutes Perry's calm voice would call from the cabin, plotting our position on the GPS, for we could see nothing of the coastline in the gathering dusk. The GPS co-ordinates took us straight on to the end of the point. Robin's job was to get us round it, though any tension he might have felt was never reflected in his voice.
>
> I was cold, tired and increasingly damp, so eventually I volunteered to make some coffee. It would at least take me below for a bit.'

We finally screeched round Cape Reykjanes at a range of a mile, not spotting the light until it was one and a half miles away, thankful yet again for the GPS, and we anchored off the west coast, as close to the beach as we dared. Our lee-way was dramatic once we turned northwards and headed in for the coast, even though it was less than a mile distant. The situation required full revs from the engine, with Chris at the helm, while the rest of us struggled to get the sixty-five-pound fisherman's anchor on deck, shackled to ten metres of chain and then attached to one of the heavy warps. Fortunately, it brought up almost immediately and we put on a spring, a line from the side of the boat to the anchor warp, to reduce sheering.

Although on an open coastline we were sheltered from the east, but as a pre-caution posted anchor watches, for the wind was certain to veer as the depression moved into the Denmark Strait. It was not a particularly happy anchorage and we moved on to a small bay when we could, but with the wind staying stubbornly southwesterly force 5-6 and a huge swell, we eventually elected to head round to Keflavik. There was no chance of leaving Iceland that Saturday. Keflavik's thermally heated open-air swimming pool enticed us all, but we ran between dips, as the wind was extremely cold. On Sunday morning Reykjavik Met Office assured us that we had another window before the next depression, so we sailed, rounding Cape Reykjanes for the fourth time in mid-afternoon, and for a while we had a superb reach before the wind backed southerly again. This time I was determined not to go backwards, so started the engine and, bashing through the seas, we made a course for Surtsey, the volcanic island which erupted into existence in the 1960s to the south of the Westermann Islands. A southeasterly force 5-6, rain and reduced visibility made our approach one I would never have chanced without the GPS, but we made a good landfall at half a mile on Surtsey and then confidently threaded our way north through the enormous stacks which extend southwards from the main island and into port. Vestmannaeyjar is the only town in the group and built close to a volcano on the island of Heimaey. The approach channel is narrow and lies between high cliffs. From the sea the town is invisible, mainly due to an eruption in 1973 when molten lava flowed into the fjord and nearly blocked the channel. The valley opens to reveal a substantial port and, although this houses only two per cent of Iceland's population, it is responsible for twelve per cent of her fish exports.

No one is sure when the islands were first inhabited, but it was certainly prior to the Viking settlement in 874 AD. The Westermann or *Vestmann*, after whom the group is named, were Irish and reputed to be monks, so the modern Icelanders point out they cannot be their descendants. However the islands have been inhabited for as long as the rest of Iceland and, between the Vikings, Barbary pirates and eruptions, have a violent history. In the meantime the port gets on with its business of harvesting the sea. We moored alongside a fishing boat in the upper part of the harbour and contacted the Harbour Master who was enormously helpful and requested a weather forecast to be faxed from the mainland. We ate ashore, noting the ubiquitous puffin on the menu but, as before, no one could face it. The puffins nest in the high cliffs surrounding the town and when the young are ready, they launch themselves. Normally, of course, puffin cliffs overhang the sea, but in Vestmannaeyjar they land all over the town as well and, although the townsfolk assured us that these youngsters were carefully collected and placed in the harbour, the presence of roast puffin on nearly every restaurant menu suggested some at least were hijacked on the way.

The forecast showed another window opening the next morning so, after filling the fuel tanks at only 50 pence a gallon, we departed, but not before the neighbouring fisherman had insisted we accept six large cod as a gift. He refused payment, but was delighted when we offered a bottle of vodka for his generosity. The fresh fish revealed the sorry fact that young people today, being supermarket fed, have no idea about gutting and cleaning. So we quickly set a trainee gutting party at work. I cooked the first batch Zulu-style, a recipe learned from the cook on my coaster in South Africa in the sixties. You place the steaks in a pan with onions, tomatoes, peppers and a little oil and allow them to broil. While admitting to bias, I find the result mouth-watering. The remaining fish was boiled and converted into fish cakes. Again, apart from Chris, none of the others had tasted anything but dry packet fish cakes and they found the moister home-made product eminently preferable. Modern shopping fashions have a lot to answer for.

As the radio was on the blink again, we were faced with no communications with the outside world until we could reach the UK shore stations via the VHF. However we made a speedy passage and four days later arrived at the Pentland Firth in fine weather before a light west nor westerly, after the sort of sailing *Suhaili* and her owner like best – reaching. The wind had been fairly constant, we were headed for only a short period, when it was sufficiently light to ignore and we pressed on under engine. But we had to cancel plans to visit the Faroes, as we were already behind schedule and everyone was due home. We had the ocean to ourselves, apart from fishing vessels on the banks and a brief flurry of naval activity due, we discovered later, to a Dutch submarine failing to report on schedule. Dolphins were frequent companions.

We slowed as we approached the Pentland Firth as there was no point in battling through against the tide. Even so there were short steep seas initially, but these eased once the tide turned eastwards and we rushed through, briefly achieving fourteen knots as the stream rose to full strength off Duncansby Head. Chris was clearly enjoying every minute of it.

'I was at the helm on watch with Robin as we approached the Pentland Firth. The waves seemed to be coming from all over the place and the wind was gusty. But I was at last getting the feel of the helm, anticipating the movement of the boat, watching the sails as much as the compass needle. It was only later that Robin told me of his doubts about letting me keep the helm in such tricky seas. A mistake, an involuntary gybe, could have damaged the mast fittings and even dismasted us, but Robin was prepared to risk that, knowing how important it was to me to have my ability trusted. It was an hour's concentrated exhilarating work with the dramatic coastline of Hoy and St John's Head towering over the breaking seas, and the shapely pillar of the Old Man of Hoy almost lost against the cliffs behind it.'

There were plenty of seals to view our spectacular progress and, unlike their Greenland relatives, they did not dive at the sight of men and boats. Instead they rose further out of the water to get a better look. These were not the only sea mammals we saw in this area, as off Aberdeen we were passed by two whales steaming north. This caused particular pleasure as there has been so much doom and gloom about North Sea contamination which has given the impression that there is nothing left alive in what was one of the richest seas anywhere in the world.

By now, of course, we were heading south and there was a growing occurrence of Channel Fever which affects any crew when they are nearing home. My only fear was in case the weather might produce a final southwesterly, as the North Sea develops a particularly nasty chop which stops *Suhaili* dead in the water when moving to windward. I had not wished to come down the North Sea for this reason, and would infinitely have preferred to sail the additional 200 miles around Ireland, but time had forced us to gamble on the shorter route. Having a fair wind all the way to the Thames would have been the equivalent of throwing all the sixes, and for a brief spell it turned southerly which reduced speed to two and a half knots. The dampening effect was apparent all round because, with an arrogance that has no place in a small boat dependent upon the wind, we had already chosen the arrival date and time, and the delay was irritating. Fortunately, the direction soon changed to the south west and continued veering northwards, so the lost time was recovered. A favourable tide swept us past the Wash to Harwich and then we were into the Thames Estuary. As the tide turned against us the wind rose from the north east and we rushed into the river, picking up the flood tide on the way which carried us to Gravesend, where we moored for the night, cleared Customs and cleaned ourselves and the boat.

On 12th September we motored quietly up river and took a temporary mooring off the Prospect of Whitby pub, as we were early for the lock at St Katharine's Dock. At this point I produced the last surprise for the crew, a bottle of Irish whiskey given to me just before we sailed from Whitehaven. I proposed a Headland which was accepted with acclamation and we sat companionably in the cockpit for the last drink aboard. I think it was James or Jim who suddenly commented that we had been together for nearly two months and there had never once been a cross word between any of us. We thought for a moment and realised it was true. We had seen new places, tried new experiences with a small team which had jelled from the start. It had been a wonderful adventure.

APPENDIX I: Greenland's Maritime Background

In the Middle Ages it was firmly believed that humans could not live at the extreme ends of the earth; it was too cold in the north and too hot in the south. Of course no one had travelled to a point where they had actually frozen or fried, but it seemed a plausible idea. Since the voyage of Pythaeas of Massilia (Marseilles), about 320 BC, it was recognised that land lay to the north of Britain, but the whereabouts of the country he called Thule is still in dispute. According to Pythaeas, Thule lay six days' sailing from the northernmost point of the British Isles, but whether he is referring to mainland Britain, or the islands to the north, is not clear. If his starting point was the mainland, then he did not reach Iceland, but perhaps the Faroes, or even Norway. If he left from the Faroes, he may indeed have sailed to Iceland. In support of the Iceland theory he tells us that Thule is one day's sail from the 'frozen sea', and this could be the first reference to Greenland pack ice.

Those magnificent but secretive seamen, the Phoenicians, operating long before Pythaeas's day, certainly traded for tin with Cornwall, probably circumnavigated the British Isles, and may have journeyed onwards to the north, but they left few records and preferred to maintain a silence to protect their commercial interests. For a thousand years after Pythaeas there are no rumours of northbound voyages although, intriguingly, Roman coins of the fourth century have been found in Iceland which might originate from a Roman British visit.

The Irish, principally monks seeking solitude, became active sailors, due to the pressure of Viking raids on their homeland. The account of St Brendan's voyage to America is only one of many such ventures and there was certainly an Irish religious colony on Iceland when the Vikings arrived. Archaeological evidence indicates there were settlers, possibly also from Ireland, in the Westermann Islands 150 years before the first confirmed reports of Viking exploration. A Latin treatise on Thule, as Iceland had by then come to be called, of about 825 AD, was based upon the personal accounts of three Irish monks. But, if the Irish went further north, there are no records and it is the Vikings who are responsible for the first description of Greenland.

The Vikings came to Iceland about 860 AD. Settlement followed swiftly and within a short space of time the two prime methods of obtaining food, farming and fishing, were well established. Around 900 AD a fisherman named

Gunnbjorn Ulfsson was swept westwards by bad weather, but managed to struggle home with the news that he had sighted some skerries, since identified as a group of rocky islets near Angmagssalik, and mountains to the west. Considering their seafaring background, it would be surprising if no one attempted to follow up Gunnbjorn's sightings during the next eighty years, but it is certain that in 978 AD, when Iceland was fully settled, a small party led by Snaebjorn Galti emigrated to eastern Greenland. They soon realised the climate was appalling and, after a miserable winter during which the would-be colonists fell out and at least one murder was committed, they returned to Iceland when weather conditions permitted.

Three or four years later, Eric the Red, banished from Iceland for three years for murder, sailed to Greenland with some companions. They had probably heard of Snaebjorn Galti's expedition, because on sighting land they turned south, rounded Cape Farewell, and spent the three-year exile exploring the west coast. Eric was so taken with the place that when his sentence was served, he returned to Iceland and advertised for colonists for what he termed a 'Green' Land – an early example of misleading public relations. He sailed with twenty-five ships, though only half reached their destination. Nevertheless the colony grew and at the height of Viking occupation amounted to around 3000 people, spread among 300 farms, with a cathedral and thirteen churches.

The Icelandic Vikings did not confine their exploration to the southern end of Greenland, and it is known that they sailed up to Spitzbergen or Svalbard (the Cold Coast). This archipelago, roughly the size of Ireland, lies only 800 miles south of the North Pole, but the surrounding waters are kept remarkably ice-free by an arm of the Gulf Stream which flows along its western seaboard. If these first-rate seamen sailed this far north, it is reasonable to assume they explored Greenland's east coast on the way, skirting the pack ice where necessary. That they did not settle there was understandable, considering the relatively good living conditions they enjoyed on the south-west coast.

The loss of the colony's independence to Norway in 1261 led to a decline, as all trade was declared a royal monopoly, and sailings were reduced to two a year. The downturn in the settlement's fortunes was also accelerated by the onset of a colder period which made any form of agriculture almost impossible. As the climate chilled, the Skraelings or Inuit, the original inhabitants who had been driven northwards by the newcomers and were better adapted to survive the conditions, gradually returned and probably killed any lingering Vikings. After the last recorded sailing in 1410, references to the region grew less frequent until it was almost forgotten, while the sea ice increased its southerly spread and effectively isolated Greenland from the rest of the world.

Other nationalities who sailed in these waters during the Middle Ages include the Genoese and Portuguese, both of whom record trading voyages to Iceland. Columbus claimed to have called in some years before he sailed to

America, although his statement that the tides had a range of ten metres would make this unlikely. The British were certainly involved in trade with the early Norse settlers and there are complaints of their piracy off Greenland in the thirteenth century. Nor did British activity cease when the Greenland colony disappeared, because mariners such as Frobisher led several expeditions which stopped at the west coast when searching for a passage to India around the north of America, as did that greatest of all Elizabethan navigators, John Davis in 1585. On a subsequent voyage in 1586, Davis divided his fleet of four into two groups, one of which investigated the region between Iceland and Greenland, the first recorded exploration of east Greenland since the Vikings.

By the beginning of the seventeenth century, there was a revival of interest in Greenland, and two Danish ships were dispatched to trace any descendants of the colonists. However, they found no sign of Norse people and the local Inuit showed no evidence of intermarriage with the settlers. At this time the Netherlands and Britain were beginning a major expansion in maritime activity. Companies were formed for trade with India, and this gave rise to fresh attempts to find alternative routes via the north-east passage around Russia. The Muscovy Company sent Henry Hudson to search for a route in 1607 and he decided to sail due north, a concept which seems strange to us, but has to be seen in the contemporary context of belief that the ice was a barrier beyond which lay open water around the North Pole, a theory which still had adherents 300 years later! He negotiated along Greenland's east coast pack ice and then crossed to Spitzbergen and achieved a latitude of 80°N, a feat which was not surpassed for another 150 years. No navigable passage was located but the presence of numerous whales to the north of Iceland quickly resulted in a thriving whaling industry, dominated by the English who did their utmost to keep out French and Dutch rivals.

A new Greenland colony was established in 1721 by a missionary, Hans Egede, and this was the start of a gradual resettlement of the west coast. The east coast was largely ignored, apart from occasional exploratory voyages and visits by whalers. It was one of the latter who bridged the gap between simple exploration and science and in 1822 discovered the fjord which bears his family name, Scoresby.

William Scoresby junior was born in 1789 and made his first whaling voyage to the Arctic with his father in 1800. The natural perils of the sea were only one of the threats to the young man's life, as it was a time of war with France. Close to Scotland on the outward voyage a French privateer bore down on them but Scoresby senior had planned for just such an emergency. The crew were concealed until the enemy was within musket shot and then a drum beat to quarters and the guns, six a side, were run out. Luckily, their antagonist, thinking he had run into a man-of-war, bore away at high speed. The season was not a profitable one, as the vessel was imprisoned in the pack ice for eight weeks and the catch was only three whales.

In 1803 Scoresby went north again and continued to do so for the next twenty years, fitting an education at Edinburgh University into the winter months. The season usually ran from April until October, with the whalers, often operating in groups, sailing along the fringe of the pack ice in search of their prey. It was a hard trade in which a youngster matured quickly. Scoresby was only sixteen when his father's vessel reached 81° 30'N, just over 500 miles short of the North Pole, a record which was to last for some time, and he was twenty-one when, in 1810, his father gave him command of the *Resolution*. Despite his youth, he returned with thirty whales, the largest cargo ever brought to Whitby.

A trade which involved the close proximity of ice was bound to be danger-ous and to encourage good seamanship. Scoresby's ship was frequently trapped and, when on one occasion he failed to extricate her by sailing through the weaker parts of a floe, he resorted to sawing through the ice to avoid seri-ous damage. Another time the ice ripped a twenty-two-foot section from the keel, and despite the advice of other captains to abandon, he managed to heel over the ship until he could remove the damaged section and fother her by hauling down a sail until it covered the hole. The hulls of the whaling ships were thick and strong, but they were no match for the tremendous forces exerted by moving ice floes.

Although Scoresby's prime purpose was whaling, he had an enquiring mind and observant nature. Early on he established that the temperature of the Arctic Sea rose as the depth increased. In 1817, frustrated by a poor season's fishing, he surveyed Jan Mayen Island. In the same year he noted a remarkable diminution of the polar ice which enabled him to sail quite close inshore in lat-itude 74°N. Over a number of seasons he charted parts of Greenland's coast, studied the local currents and their influence on iceberg movements, and landed when time permitted. It may seem strange that other whalers were incurious about the land lying to the west of the fishing grounds, but the cap-tains were concentrating on the business in hand and there was no commercial advantage to be gained by risking ships on a coastline so frequently sealed by ice. It was on one of his investigative trips that Scoresby came across the huge fjord which he named after his father.

The curious phenomenon of abnormal refraction experienced in high lati-tudes would have been observed by seamen for centuries, but Scoresby wrote one of the first descriptions of it. Light rays are bent when they pass between one medium and another of different optical density and the effect of rays passing through the atmosphere close to the horizon is to elevate it and allow objects to be seen that should be out of sight. In high latitudes this refraction can distort, so that a chunky iceberg can appear as a thin sticklike object or float in the air above the horizon.

Scoresby's work was the beginning of a gradual international programme to survey the whole east Greenland coast. Cape Parry to the Haystack, approximately 72°-75°N, was examined by Lieutenant Foster of the *Gripper* in 1823. Lieutenant de Blossville arrived with a French expedition in 1833 on the *Lilloise*. He sent a report from Iceland to the Geographical Society in Paris but was lost on his return voyage to Greenland to resume work. His name is memorialised on the coast south of Scoresby Sound. The coast was equally inhospitable to the next major expedition from Germany in 1869 led by Captain Koldewey. With two vessels, the *Germania* and *Hansa*, he sailed north of Haystack and named Germania Land, an extensive and frequently ice-free area, but not for the *Hansa*, which was crushed in the ice and the survivors travelled to the south coast on a journey of quite incredible hardship.

The Danes, who always had a latent interest in Greenland, sent an expedition to the south coast in 1829 under Captain Graah. Captain Gustav Holm followed in 1884 and found a way through the ice to Angmagssalik where there was a flourishing Inuit colony with whom he over-wintered. Another Danish expedition, led by Lieutenant Ryder, spent a winter in Scoresby Sound in 1891-2 and ten years later Amdrup and Einer Mikkelsen surveyed the coast between Angmagssalik and Scoresby Sound in a small boat. Ice prevented them from entering Kangerdlugssuaq Fjord, but the fjord that flows into its mouth is named after Amdrup and we considered this as a possible anchorage in 1991.

If the area were not so vast, it would have been crowded over the next few years. The American, Peary, crossed the Greenland Icecap in 1892 and again in 1895. Four years later the Swede, Nathorst, explored between Scoresby Sound and Shannon Island, about 75°N, where there was evidence of earlier Inuit encampments. P. Dusen produced the first large-scale chart of the area between Davy Sound and Foster Bight, approximately 72°- 73°N. The following year Peary was back and reached Cape Clarence Wyckoff, 82°N, while, separately, I. Koch surveyed between Scoresby and Davy Sounds. More detailed knowledge of this coastline was obtained by the Due d'Orleans in 1905. However, attention was now shifting to the South Pole and there was only one more expedition before the First World War, when Mylius Erichsen completed the survey from Pendulum Island northwards in 1906-8. Although one might expect this concentrated activity to have produced excellent charts for the whole east coast, the ice made this impossible and there are still large tracts where data is superficial and where, as the *Admiralty Pilot* would say, 'Mariners should exercise extreme caution.'

Our interest focused on the area in and around Kangerdlugssuaq Fjord where there was a lack of historical information. The first real exploration by Europeans had not been until 1930 when Gino Watkins took Shackleton's *Quest* along the coast to set up a weather station with a view to establishing if an air route were feasible and, at the same time, they added to Amdrup's survey. Names from Wager's team, Watkins, Courtauld, Chapman, were to become familiar to us in our travels, as many of the major features around the fjord were named after them. They started at Angmagssalik where a base camp and radio station were established and manned by Lemon. Here was another significant name, since the Cathedral lies in the Lemon Mountains. *Quest* encountered heavy sea ice off the coast during mid-August and was obliged to retreat to sea for clear water. They noted the movement of ice in the swell and that when waves broke against the large bergs the spray was thrown as high as their masts. Eventually *Quest* was manoeuvred through the coastal ice belt right into Kangerdlugssuaq Fjord and anchored in the north-western corner. While the survey team operated from a small boat, *Quest* sailed round to neighbouring Mikis Fjord to fly off an aeroplane for an aerial survey. In fact *Quest* had only a short stay in Kangerdlugssuaq before her captain decided it was late in the season and it would be advisable to head south. Since then it appears little surveying has been carried out, and the maps we used for our journey were based on Watkins' work.

APPENDIX II: Expeditions to the Kangerdlugssuaq Area

Greenland is not only the largest island in the world, it also has the second largest icecap, dwarfed only by the continent of Antarctica. Most of Greenland is covered by a featureless dome of ice, which in places is 3,000 metres (9,000 feet) thick. Gigantic glaciers, fed by the Icecap, flow down to the sea, carving out deep-cut fjords and exposing the mountains which cling to the coastline. Their shape and character are determined by the nature of the rock, the hard granite and gneiss yielding dramatic rock aiguilles, while the softer basalt presents more rounded domes that are often covered in snow. The highest and steepest of these peaks are on the east coast from Angmagssalik, at 66°N, to just north of Scoresby Sound at 73°N.

The early climbing in Greenland was on the west coast which is much easier to reach because the Gulf Stream flows up through the Davis Strait, rendering it fairly free of ice. Edward Whymper, who made the first ascent of the Matterhorn and was the most famous of all Victorian mountaineers, visited west Greenland in 1867 and 1872. The Icecap itself was first crossed by Nansen in 1888 and it was in 1870 that Lieutenant Payer, with Professor Copeland and Peter Ellinger, made the first ascent of a 7,000 foot (2,150 metre) peak above Franz Josef Fjord in the Scoresby area, later known as Payer Peak. This was to be the highest peak climbed in Greenland for the next fifty years. From its summit they discerned an even higher peak which Payer described as 'a monstrous pyramid of ice to the west, rising about 4,850 feet above a high mountain ridge,' and they named it Petermanns Peak after their expedition leader.

In 1929 a Cambridge University expedition explored the region and attempted the peak. Combining scientific research with exploration and mountaineering, it set the pattern for most of the expeditions that followed. The climbing party of six included Augustine Courtauld, who was to feature prominently in Greenland history, and the young Vivien Fuchs, who was to lead the Commonwealth Trans-Antarctic Expedition in 1957-8. Because they opted to back-pack rather than haul sledges they whittled their loads down to the minimum, their heaviest single item being a theodolite weighing twenty pounds with its tripod, a token of their devotion to science. It took them a week of hard slogging to reach Petermanns Peak, and it was Forbes, Wakefield and Varley who reached the summit in deteriorating conditions and a savage wind.

The following year Gino Watkins' British Arctic Air Route expedition established its weather station on the Greenland Icecap, and explored the coastline
to the north of Angmagssalik, reaching Kangerdlugssuaq from the sea for the
first time, and gaining a glimpse from their plane of a range of mountains to
the north of Kangerdlugssuaq that appeared to be higher than any seen so far
in Greenland. They also had a climbing objective. Up to this time a mountain
to the north of Angmagssalik, Mount Forel, at around 11,200 feet (3,414 metres),
was believed to be the highest in Greenland. Watkins' original plan had been
to use the expedition Tiger Moth to land on the glacier immediately below the
peak. This would have represented the first use of aircraft in mountaineering
but, on discovering the fierceness of the winter winds, they abandoned the
project. Their team for a first attempt in March comprised Spencer Chapman,
later to make the first ascent of Chomolhari in Tibet, Lawrence Wager, who
was to go on to attempt Everest, and Stephenson, who had never set foot on
ice or rock before. They hoped to sledge along the edge of the Icecap to
Kangerdlugssuaq and climb Mount Forel on the way, but they were stopped
by deep snows and bitter cold less than half way to Forel.

They returned in May, with Bingham taking Chapman's place and, in warmer
weather with better snow conditions, made good progress, taking thirteen
days to cover the 176 miles to the foot of the mountain. They reached a height
of 10,500 feet (3,200 metres) but were stopped by a dome of hard steep ice. In
the days of straight-picked ice axes and step-cutting it would have taken too
long to hack their way to the summit, so they consoled themselves with boil-
ing their hypsometer, reading their aneroids and determining that they had
climbed higher within the Arctic Circle than anyone had climbed before.

Wager was so fascinated by the geology of the Kangerdlugssuaq area that he
returned with his brother on a brief visit in 1932 when they first noticed a high
peak in the distance above the Frederiksborg Glacier which they called
Cathedral Mountain.

In 1933-4 a three-man expedition attempted to reach and survey the mountains to the north-east of Kangerdlugssuaq sighted by Watkins. The driving
force was Martin Lindsay, a regular soldier in the Royal Scots Fusiliers, who
had been a member of Watkins' team, and who, after Watkins' tragic death in a
kayaking accident, wanted to complete the work they had started and climb
the Monarch, as the highest peak in the range had been named. Since he could
not afford to charter a boat, he planned to make his approach from the more
easily accessible west coast, sledging with dog teams across the Icecap to what
we now call the Watkins Mountains, and then travelling down to Angmagssalik,
surveying all the way. It would make it the longest unsupported sledge journey
ever and was very much a forerunner of the modern lightweight expedition.

They accomplished the 1,080 miles in 103 days, a remarkable achievement in
view of the relative inexperience of the other two members of the team and

the slenderness of the rations on which they survived, twenty-one ounces a day, augmented in the face of insurrection by four ounces of dog pemmican. Lindsay had not realised the importance of fat in a survival diet when he reduced the margarine ration. But pemmican does make an excellent base for a thick stew and is something that is very difficult to get hold of today. Modern dehydrated foods are harder to digest and not nearly so nutritious.

They were ravenously hungry most of the time, had a narrow escape with a tent fire and, on reaching the Watkins Mountains, were far too over-extended to contemplate a diversion to climb the Monarch. They therefore turned south, skirting the peaks on the edge of the Icecap, surveying all the way, to look down on the end of Kangerdlugssuaq where they sighted 'a new and very fine mountain range, Alpine in appearance, some of the peaks being like the aiguilles around Chamonix'. These must have been the Lemon Mountains.

In 1935 Wager was back in east Greenland. Since his last visit he had been on Everest in 1933, reaching the high point at that time of over 28,000 feet (8,535 metres). He was well funded, had been able to charter a boat to take his expedition in to the east coast, and was planning to spend the winter there to give him a full year to carry out a thorough geological and natural sciences survey of the Kangerdlugssuaq area. Being a climber, he also planned to climb the highest peak in the Watkins Mountains, which would now seem to be the highest point in Greenland. In his team was Jack Longland, another member of the 1933 Everest expedition and one of the most talented young rock climbers in Britain. Expeditioning tended to be a male preserve, but Wager decided to bring out with him some of the wives of team members to take an active part in proceedings. The Inuit they employed also had their families with them and Wager commented on how well it all worked.

The team sailed once again in *Quest*, reaching Angmagssalik on 16th July after a fierce struggle with pack ice. They sailed up the coast a few days later, leaving a party on the Skærgård Peninsula to build the winter quarters, then six of them, including Lawrence Wager, his brother H.G. Wager, Augustine Courtauld and Jack Longland, re-embarked on *Quest* to sail up to Wiedermann Fjord from where they planned to sledge into the Watkins Mountains. The floe ice was too heavy, however, and they could only get a short way to the north into J.C. Jacobsen Fjord. This meant a very much longer approach, but they were undismayed, following the Schjelderup Glacier and then the snow-clad hills flanking the Sorgenfri Glacier, until they could cross it and gain the huge Christian IV Glacier which led them in to the Watkins Mountains after fifteen hard days man-hauling their sledges. The highest peak at 12,139 feet (3,700 metres), now named Gunnbjorns Fjeld, was comparatively easy, 'an anti-climax... only an interlude in fifteen days of fascinating mountain travel', in Longland's words when he described the climb in the *Alpine Journal*, but it was to be nearly forty years before it was repeated. The journey to it had been a brilliant piece of navigation, across complex mountain country, helped by the map drawn from the aerial survey of Watkins' expedition.

Those who had only come out for the summer season now set sail with *Quest*, leaving Wager with a party of seven which included his brother and their wives, to winter in Kangerdlugssuaq, from where, with the aid of the air survey map, they reconnoitred a route on to the Frederiksborg Glacier via a parallel glacier which they named Bye Glacier (now called Sidegletscher). This led comparatively easily on to the Frederiksborg Glacier above the heavily crevassed lower section. Wager wrote in the *Geographical Journal*:

> 'We could see about five miles off the highest peak of the neighbourhood (8,450 feet) which my brother and I, in 1932, had called Cathedral Mountain, and to the east the two astonishingly symmetrical aiguilles, which we had called by the Eskimo name of Mitiwanga (breasts). This mountain group formed of the gneisses of the Metamorphic Complex is the finest in the whole Kangerdlugssuaq region, and has a more attractive shape than the higher Watkins Mountains of Rasmussen Land. For the mountaineer they would provide difficult rock-climbing problems like those of the Chamonix Aiguilles.'

Early in January 1936, when Watkins Fjord was well frozen, they were able to use dog teams to carry half a ton of food up Sidegletscher and the Frederiksborg Glacier to a dump opposite the Cathedral, ready for a series of successful spring and summer journeys up on to the Icecap. Wager had decided against taking any radios with him, commenting on his plans for their return:

> 'Arrangements had been made through Dr. Hoel of Oslo for a sealing vessel to fetch us, if ice permitted, between August 15 and 25. If bad ice prevented this, reasonable attempts were to be made later, but should these fail we were to be left until the following year. We had taken food and fuel to make a second year possible, and indeed with the help of the Eskimo it should have been reasonably comfortable, so that I had made it clear before Courtauld left in 1935 that we did not wish any expensive or dangerous attempts to be made to fetch us away.
>
> We had no wireless apparatus, apart from a time signal wireless on which we occasionally heard scraps of news. This was a definite policy; it would have involved much extra work and have been costly to have had reliable wireless communication. Our main reason however for not including it in our equipment was that the expedition would be a self-contained unit not

needing any help from outside, and indeed not being able to get it during ten months of the year.'

Very different from today, when the Danish government insist on all expeditions carrying an emergency radio beacon and when, in the event of having to activate it, there is a good chance that a rescue helicopter or even a ski-equipped plane could fly in within a few hours. In extremis one would be all too glad of the rescue, and yet I cannot help regretting the introduction of these government-enforced safety measures. They reduce the fundamental element of adventure which dictates the kind of self-sufficiency that Croft and Lindsay or Wager and his team accepted on their journeys.

The still unclimbed Mount Forel remained another attractive target for exploration in the Schweizerland region. Where Gino Watkins had failed, a Swiss expedition led by the brilliant climber, André Roch, reached Angmagssalik in July 1938, travelled by motor boat to the head of Sermilik Fjord and then, with the help of eight Inuit and their dog teams, reached and climbed Mount Forel. The war put a stop to further mountain exploration, though German U-boats and weather ships lurked in the Greenland fjords and the Denmark Strait became an important route for surface raiders.

After the war the tempo of climbing and exploration hotted up. The Staunings Alps, by Scoresby Sound, closely resemble Chamonix granite and became particularly popular through the late fifties and sixties, being developed as an alpine rock playground. Schweizerland was also extensively explored and climbed, but the Lemon Mountains were ignored until 1972 when a Westminster School party set out for Kangerdlugssuaq, choosing it because it was less frequented than the other areas. This expedition was typical of many going to Greenland up to the present day, the majority being from either schools or universities, with a scientific as well as a sporting objective.

The driving force was Stan Woolley who was to become an expert on Greenland travel. By this time Greenland was more accessible and they were able to fly from Iceland to a USAF base at Kulusuk on an island off Angmagssalik, where they were collected by an old supply boat, the *Polarbjorn*, a converted trawler of 460 tons. They squeezed aboard with two Inuit families, complete with their boats, huskies and a year's supplies, some Danes on their way to a met station and a young English geologist, Kent Brooks, who was making a major survey of the Kangerdlugssuaq region that has continued to the present day. From a base near the Inuit settlement on the Skærgård Peninsula the team carried out an extensive glaciological and botanical programme before seven of them set out on a journey up the Frederiksborg Glacier. No one had been there since Wager in 1936. It took them four days to back-pack across the hills on the western side of the lower part of the glacier, then up to the foot of the Lemon Mountains. On 16th August they tackled the dramatically steep pair of peaks that Wager had named Mitiwanga (Mitivagkat on the Danish map), climbing a snow gully leading up to the col between them and then on up to the left-hand summit over rocky slabs and ribbons of snow. As C.D. Campbell, the climbing leader, described it in their expedition report:

> 'A short snowfield provided the classic end to the route, as the summit appeared inch by inch over the snowy skyline. I think we ran the last few feet, and there we were, a perfect untouched summit of 2,250 metres, with the frowning ranks of all those still untouched mountains peering through the drifting snow. A couple of birds above us protested at our invasion, and the ice cap stretched unbroken to the horizon and way beyond.
>
> But sitting there with this all around didn't satisfy our more basic needs for long and Kendal Mint Cake, Rum Candy and, I hesitate to mention, even a Primus appeared. We brewed up in the Ryvita tin, feeling a vague sense of the absurd at six Englishmen sipping tea.'

The Lemon Mountains were not to have another visit until we arrived in 1991, though there was plenty of geological activity on the coast around Kangerdlugssuaq. Kent Brooks, whom the Westminster party met on their way to the fjord, visited the Skærgård Peninsula regularly for the next twenty years, carrying out a detailed survey of the Skærgård Intrusion which proved to be an Aladdin's cave of minerals, including gold and platinum. Not only university field parties were now interested. A Canadian mining company called Platanova started an exhaustive survey, building an air strip at Sodalen at the head of Mikis Fjord. They have discovered gold, though the price of gold would have to be sufficiently high to justify the costs of extraction. The proportion of gold in the rocks is in the region of five parts in a million, which would mean crushing and dumping a huge quantity of rock to extract the precious metal.

Should commercial extraction start, it would mean a town of some 3,000 people being built with all the risks of pollution and the resultant scars that mining would inevitably leave. This might seem unjustifiable on environmental grounds, but Greenland is not an uninhabited wilderness like Antarctica. It has its population of some 40,000 Greenlanders who are of mixed blood, and around 10,000 Europeans who have settled there. The country is a self-governing province of Denmark with its own parliament. But its economy, based on hunting and fishing, is precarious. A successful gold mine would be a major boost, making the country less dependent on Denmark and bringing valuable revenue and employment, though I suspect the majority of the workers would be brought in from abroad. A small town and even an extensive mine would be lost in the vast mountain mass of the Kangerdlugssuaq region. The Frederiksborg Glacier and Lemon Mountains would not even be affected, though they would become very much more accessible.

I cannot help regretting the thought that this rugged and empty coastline should suffer such commercial development and yet, at the same time, it is important to understand and sympathise with the needs of the Greenland people. If mining does come to this area, one can only hope and campaign for an impact that does the minimum damage to the environment.

Stan Woolley returned to the area in 1987, with Robin Illingworth, Rob Ferguson and Steve McCabe to make the third ascent of Gunnbjorns Fjeld in the Watkins Mountains (the second having been made by Alistair Allen's party in 1971). Woolley's original plan had been more ambitious. They had hoped to land on the plateau, using a ski-equipped twin-engine Otter, climb Gunnbjorns Fjeld, and then sledge down to Mount Forel and climb that. The ski landing had to be ruled out, however, and they ended up landing at Sodalen at the head of Mikis Fjord. They succeeded on Gunnbjorns Fjeld but abandoned their plans for the long sledge journey down to Mount Forel and Schweizerland.

The following year, 1988, the British found a satisfactory spot to land an air-craft and as a result the Watkins Mountains were flung open to a series of expeditions. The Swede, Ingemar Olsson, climbed Gunnbjorns Fjeld and claimed two other high peaks known as the Cone and the Dome, which he believed were higher and which he renamed Ingemars Fjeld and Lars Fjeld after himself and his partner. The Danish Polar Institute refused to uphold either the claimed heights or the nomenclature, the latter because no feature in Greenland can be named after a living person.

Jim Lowther, with a team of six, which included Allen Jewhurst and Jan Pester, climbed Gunnbjorns Fjeld, the Cone and the Dome just a week later, as well as several more unclimbed peaks in the region. Jim had served a thor-ough apprenticeship in Greenland travel and mountaineering, having visited Greenland for the first time in 1982 as a member of a British Schools' Exploring Society expedition. He returned in 1983 and 1985 and in 1986 co-led a univer-sity expedition to Schweizerland, exploring new ground and making the first British ascent of Mount Forel. By this time he had become a Greenland addict, attracted by the spacious emptiness of the place. He was committed to the use of the pulk, a one-man sledge with a rigid trace, as opposed to the classic Nansen sledge which was hauled by three or four people, pulling on tradi-tional traces. In 1987 he and his partner, Nick Hulton, made a particularly fast parachute-assisted traverse of the Icecap from Angmagssalik to Sondrestrom Fjord. In 1988, a Swedish party of four, led by Bengt Rodin, succeeded in mak-ing the journey that Stan Woolley had planned the previous year, climbing both Gunnbjorns Fjeld and Mount Forel.

Jim Lowther returned in 1990, joining a larger party led by the veteran Stan Woolley, to explore and climb in the area to the west of Kangerdlugssuaq. The nine-man team had a wide age range with members who had been in Woolley's expeditions to Kangerdlugssuaq going back to 1972. It split into two groups on lines of age, the younger team going for unclimbed peaks, and making nine first ascents in as many days, while the older group combined a more modest mountaineering programme with some scientific work.

The Lemon Mountains were therefore in 1991 the one remaining major range that was still almost untouched, with the Cathedral, described by Stan Woolley as the most attractive unclimbed peak in Greenland, awaiting some-one's attention. It was an attractive objective indeed.

APPENDIX III: Suhaili Bugt, A Hydrographic Survey by Perry Crickmere and James Burdett

This survey was carried out from the yacht *Suhaili* by Perry Crickmere and James Burdett in August 1991. We were members of Robin Knox-Johnston and Chris Bonington's sailing/climbing expedition to Kangerdlugssuaq. The coastal outline and topographical features were taken from a previous survey of reliable origin and enlarged to fit our scale. Positions were fixed by GPS satellite navigation system and double checked; basic surveying instruments and techniques were otherwise used throughout. All soundings were taken with a lead and line.

Directions

Approaching from the south: Head for the rounded peak of Kraemer Island (the peak isn't on this chart, but is one and a half miles northwest of Suhaili Bugt). Leave the Skærgård Peninsula and nearby islands, of which Mellem is the most northerly, at least four cables to starboard, thus avoiding off-lying skerries. To starboard the sheer mountains of the mainland are interrupted by Forbindelses Gletscher (Connecting Glacier) which is the largest glacier in view and the only one which reaches the sea on this stretch of coast; as Mellem comes abeam a large conical mountain appears to rise up in the saddle formed by Connecting Glacier (it is some distance beyond the glacier itself). When this peak bears 70° true alter course to starboard and approach the entrance to Suhaili Bugt (between Mellem and Kraemer). Three islets lie in the entrance, leave the first two to starboard and the third to port. Shoals extend from these, as marked, and cover at high tide. Inside the anchorage there are no significant dangers but, if continuing through into Uttental Sound, give the islets to the north of Lille Mellem a wide berth, as these also shoal.

Shelter

The bay is open only to the south-west, and the exposure from this point is minimised by the islands of Mellem and Lille Mellem. Kraemer Island affords good protection from west, through north, round to south-east; although the pitarac, a sudden and sometimes violent offshore wind which builds up in unsettled weather, could be compounded by the funnelling effect of some of the gullies, we didn't encounter anything over F2-3 while we were there. The mouth of Kangerdlugssuaq was often shrouded in fog but Suhaili Bugt seemed to be far enough inland to be immune most of the time.

Holding

Mostly thick mud where it's shallow enough to anchor. We found very good holding at the north-east corner of the bay (two fishermen and a stern line ashore, although there is swinging room).

Tides

Tidal height was measured over the two weeks between 2-16 August 1991. Chart datum is one-foot below the lowest observed height. The largest observed range of tide was nine-foot. Currents around Mellem and Lille Mellem set north-east on the flood and southwest on the ebb and are reasonably strong as Uttental Sound drains out past these islands. We didn't take any accurate current measurements as such.

Ice

Local ice conditions were very variable and depended a lot on tidal currents. Most of the large bergs tended to go aground out in the fjord; those that drew little enough to get in usually hung around for several days, gradually breaking up and melting. We had to move *Suhaili* once to avoid a berg of fifty-foot diameter.

The ice conditions in 1991 were apparently very mild so our experiences are probably by no means typical.

Variation

The predominant variation of this part of eastern Greenland is 31°W (dec.12'E annually). However, observations we made produced wildly different figures, including at one point a 9°E variation! It's possible that our calculations are erroneous but we did check them several times. A possible explanation is the effect of the Skærgård Intrusion which forms a large part of Kraemer Island and the nearby mainland. It is a magma intrusion which pushed up from beneath the crust relatively recently and might have a magnetic alignment of its own.

Unsurveyed area

The area between Lille Mellem and Mellem wasn't sounded. Small bergs regularly grounded here, so it may be quite shallow in places.

Local settlement

There is an Inuit settlement close by on the Skærgård Peninsula. It has about ten semi-permanent huts and is used mainly as a summer hunting camp, though one family we met planned to spend the winter there as well.

Fresh water

Mostly snow melt streams, the three marked on the chart provided a good supply.

Sailing Glossary

AUTOHELM A British make of automatic pilot, which can be used to steer the boat and thus relieve the helmsman from this task.

BOBSTAY A chain that runs from the end of the bowsprit to the boat's stem or cutwater. It is designed to hold the end of the bowsprit down against the upward pull of the forestay which holds the mast in position.

CLOSE-HAULED The act of sailing a vessel as close as possible into the direction from which the wind is coming without the sails flapping. This is also known as beating into the wind.

CQR ANCHOR A type of anchor, introduced just before World War Two, which is shaped like two plough shares set back to back. It has considerably greater holding power for its weight than a conventional anchor on all bottoms except rock.

FETCH The distance of open water crossed by waves before they reach the vessel or the shore.

FISHERMAN ANCHOR The conventional curved anchor with its stock set at right-angles to heavy flukes. The stock lies flat on the ocean bed forcing the flukes upright so that they try to dig in. It holds well on rocky bottoms but not as well as more modern anchors in sand and mud.

FOTHERING A method of stopping a leak in a vessel by drawing a sheet of canvas over the area of the leak so that water pressure holds it close against the vessel side and reduces the leak.

FREEBOARD The distance between the ship's deck and the water surface.

GYBE The action of turning a vessel through the wind downwind so that, when completed, the wind is blowing across the vessel from the opposite side to where it was at the start. In a yacht it means taking the booms and sails across from one side to another and, since they swing across a considerable distance, the action can cause damage if uncontrolled.

GPS The Global Positioning System. A satellite navigation system that uses a number of satellites in orbit to obtain a fix. The latest systems, which were developed by the US Army, update the position every twenty seconds or so and are generally reckoned to be accurate to within eighty metres anywhere in the world.

HALYARD The wire or rope used to hoist a sail. On large yachts it is usually lead to a winch for greater power.

HAND To handle an item, usually used to refer to bringing something in such as the log-line or a sail.

HEADLAND (1) A conspicuous point of land sticking out into the sea.

HEADLAND (2) An arbitrary celebration aboard *Suhaili,* used when the crew, skipper and owner, who each have one vote, are in agreement that something special has happened. It can be the rounding of a real Headland but is more often any event that occurs during the voyage that everyone thinks should be recognised by a drink.

JIB A triangular fore and aft sail set on a forestay of the fore mast in a vessel.

KATABATIC WIND When air is cooled at night or by contact with a cold surface, it becomes more dense and will tend to flow towards lower ground. Often it accelerates down valleys creating a powerful offshore wind.

LEE Generally means shelter, thus one can sail into the lee of a headland and find shelter from the wind. A lee shore, however, is on the lee or sheltered side of a vessel and therefore a shore on to which the wind is blowing and therefore dangerous to a vessel since the wind will tend to blow her on to it.

LEEWARD The direction at sea downwind of a vessel, as opposed to upwind which is known as windward.

LEEWAY The distance that a vessel is set downwind of her course by the action of wind.

MIZEN or MIZZEN The name of the aftermost mast in some sailing vessel rigs such as a ketch like *Suhaili.*

REACH Sailing a vessel with the sails full and the wind free. A vessel sailing close hauled or running before the wind would not be reaching.

SEA-ROOM Space in which to manoeuvre. A vessel can have plenty of sea-room if she is well off-shore, but little sea-room when close into a shore, particularly a lee shore.

SPINNAKER A three-cornered lightweight sail, set forward of a mast, and used to increase the sail area when the vessel is sailing downwind.

SPREADERS The struts that extend in pairs either side of a mast to spread the angle of the upper rigging, called shrouds, so that they provide better support.

STERN GLAND A bearing, through which the propeller shaft passes between the inside of a vessel and the sea. It usually has a gland on it which may be tightened around the propeller shaft so that the shaft may rotate but ingress of water is kept to a minimum.

WARPS Rope used for warping or moving a vessel from one position in a harbour or anchorage to another. They are usually among the heaviest and largest carried by a vessel.

WINDAGE The parts of a vessel that catch the wind, usually referring to the superstructure, masts and rigging.

Climbing Glossary

ABSEILING Method of descending a rock face by sliding down a rope, usually doubled so that it can be pulled down afterwards.

BELAY A method of safeguarding a climbing partner from falling by tying oneself to a firm anchor from which one can pay out or take in the rope.

BERGSCHRUND The gap or crevasse between the glacier proper and the upper snows of a face.

BIVOUAC To spend a night in the open or in a snow hole on a mountain, or in a minimal bivvy sack or tent, as opposed to a proper tent or fixed camp.

BUTTRESS A rock protrusion between two gullies.

CHIMNEY A fissure in the rock or ice wide enough to climb up inside.

CLIMBING GRADES Systems of stating the degree of difficulty of a climb. The terminology varies between climbing nations. Britain started with descriptive grades of Easy, Moderate, Difficult, Very Difficult, Severe, Very Severe (VS), Extremely Severe; with further distinctions afforded by prefixing Mild and Hard, e.g. HVS Hard Very Severe. Scottish Grade V is Severe to Very Severe.

CIRQUE An arc of mountains round the headwall of a valley or glacier.

COL A pass or dip in a ridge usually between two peaks.

CORRIE A hollow at the head of a hanging valley.

CRAMPONS Steel spiked frames which can be fitted to boots to give grip on ice and firm snow slopes.

CREVASSE A crack in a glacier surface which can be both wide and very deep, made by the movement of the glacier over the irregular shapes in its bed, or by bends in its course.

FAULT LINES Natural fracture lines in a rock face which offer a route to the climber.

FIGURE-OF-EIGHT DESCENDEUR A metal device used in abseiling.

FRIEND A spring-loaded camming device, with a point of attachment for a rope, which jams in a rock crack and offers protection.

FRONT-POINTING Climbing straight up steep snow or ice by means of kicking in the front point of crampons and supporting balance with an ice axe, or, on steep ground, using the picks of an ice axe and ice hammer in either hand.

GENDARMES Rock pinnacles obtruding from a ridge, often surrounded by snow.

GULLY The recess between two buttresses; under ice or snow conditions, a natural avalanche channel.

HAND-JAM Wedging the hand in a crack to establish a hold.

ICEFALL Where a glacier falls steeply and creates a series of crevasses and pinnacles of ice.

ICE SCREW A climbing aid which is screwed into the ice and to which a kara-biner and rope are attached to form a belay or abseil point.

KARABINER Oval metal snap-links used for, among other things, attaching rope to an anchor.

MORAINE Accumulation of stones and debris carried down by a glacier.

NORDIC SKIING Cross-country skiing.

NUTS Originally were nuts (of nuts and bolts) with the thread drilled out, but progressed to alloy wedges. Used in cracks to support belays.

PEGS Metal spikes which are hammered into a rock crack to support a belay. Also called *pitons* (French).

PITCH Section of climbing between two stances or belay points.

PRUSIKING A method of directly ascending a rope with the aid of prusik knots, or friction hitches, with foot loops.

RIDGE The line along which two faces of a mountain meet.

ROPING UP When two or more climbers tie in to a rope in order to belay each other over difficult ground.

SERAC Wall, pinnacle or tower of ice, often unstable and dangerous.

SCREE Loose rock debris that has collected at the base of a mountain slope.

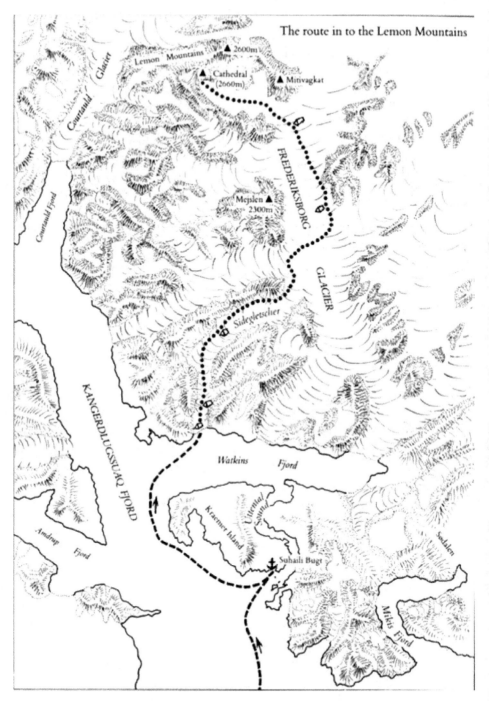

The route in to the Lemon Mountains

THE ROUTE IN TO THE LEMON MOUNTAINS

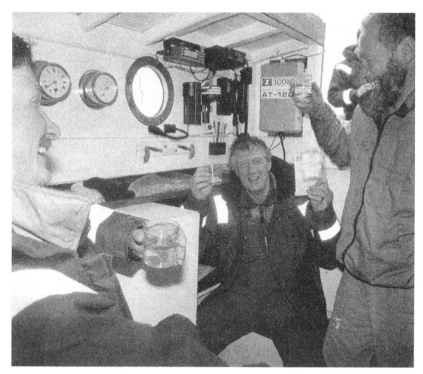

A serious excuse for a headland, as Perry and Robin help John Dunn celebrate becoming a grandfather.

Happy Hour, left to right, Chris, Perry, Robin, James, John, Jim.

Jim Lowther stitching Chris up after he had missed an onion.

Washing the salt out of our oilskins in Reykjavik harbour while waiting to be cleared through Customs.

What the experts tell you not to do is pay a social call on an iceberg. But there are times when curiosity gets the better of discretion.

All one afternoon we sailed towards a real beauty of an iceberg, and eventually *Suhaili* was dwarfed by a floating mass heavier than any man-made creation.

Robin administering vodka externally to disinfect his blisters at the end of a hard day in harness.

Robin trying to navigate Kangerdlugssuaq Fjord from Gino Watkins' 1930 aerial survey.
The climbing party arrives at the foot of the Cathedral.

The climbing party arrives at the foot of the Cathedral.

At our first camp ashore where we landed the gear from *Suhaili* for our journey on to the Cathedral.

A surprise birthday party at our Sidegletscher camp.

Jan and Allen hauling their pulks up the immensity of the Frederiksborg Glacier with a line of unnamed, unclimbed peaks beyond.

Encouraged by Robin, Allen leaps one of the deep surface streams which bedevilled our progress up the Frederiksborg Glacier.

The Cathedral. We climbed the left-hand fork of the wide ice gully to the col and then followed the skyline to the left-hand top.

A very wet and tired Chris near the end of the Sidegletscher on the return journey.

Chris climbing the rock ridge below Robin's Pinnacle on the second attempt.

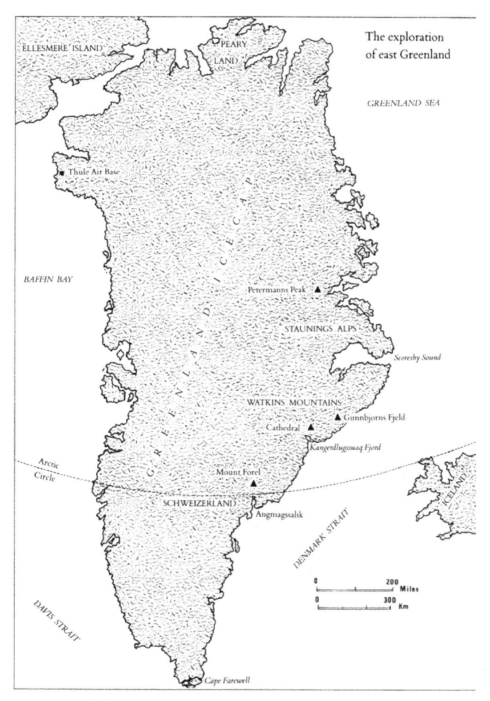

The exploration
of east Greenland

GREENLAND SEA

ELLESMERE ISLAND

PEARY
LAND

Thule Air Base

BAFFIN BAY

G R E E N L A N D   I C E C A P

Petermanns Peak ▲

STAUNINGS ALPS

Scoresby Sound

WATKINS MOUNTAINS

▲ Gunnbjorns Fjeld

Cathedral ▲

Kangerdlugssuaq Fjord

Arctic
Circle

Mount Forel
▲

ICELAND

SCHWEIZERLAND

Angmagssalik

DENMARK STRAIT

0		200
		Miles
0		300
		Km

DAVIS STRAIT

Cape Farewell

THE EXPLORATION OF EAST GREENLAND

SUHAILI BUGT

Printed in the USA
CPSIA information can be obtained
at www.ICGtesting.com
JSHW012017140824
68134JS00025B/2462

9 781912 560523